OF WESTLAKE

A Documentary Assembled
by ENRIQUE LOPEZ

G. P. PUTNAM'S SONS, New York

FOR MILLIE,
with gratitude for her advice and sympathy

Contents

1771580

Foreword

WHEN I first read the opening chapters of *Seven Wives of Westlake,* my immediate response was outright indignation and a total refusal to admit I had ever known the kind of people who appear in this book—certainly not the patients in my practice, or my friends. I had assumed that my people (and I use that term loosely) were more resourceful, independent, self-sufficient, and basically more sure of themselves.

Then, as I started wondering why I had reacted so strongly, I came to realize that these rap sessions had raised my own consciousness with respect to the harsh fundamental problems that confront millions of women who, at every level of our society, find themselves in a state of bewilderment, confusion, anger, and desperation. Rereading those initial chapters, I could actually feel the frantic urgency of their search for an "out." And as each successive page brought to mind the early phases of my own development—from childhood to adolescence, my years in college and graduate school, subsequent marriage and motherhood—my compassion for these particular women increased and deepened, knowing that they, too, were becoming painfully aware of the isolation, frustration, and alienation which even the most gifted and favored women have been confronting (and sometimes overcoming) since time immemorial.

With brutal frankness, occasional despair, and mo-

7

ments of wit and wisdom, these seven wives offer a disturbing picture of women yearning and struggling for economic independence, personal identification, sexual satisfaction or adjustment, creative expression, familial stability, and a host of other individual expectations. But as one sees them pick and pry into their own psyches, one is inevitably aware that men face many of the same problems, though in different ways. What, after all, is strictly male or female?

Though fascinated by most of the book, I was especially impressed by the disturbingly poignant chapters on "Children" and "On Growing Old." Many women will freely admit hating and resenting their parents, their husbands, their brothers and sisters, their closest friends, but they simply cannot bring themselves to admit they sometimes hate and resent their own children and perhaps wish they had never had them— not even to their most intimate friends or to a psychotherapist. For such hatred is the ultimate taboo for a mother, an admission of the worst kind of personal failure and unworthiness. But these women, somehow trusting each other in a veritable spasm of naked honesty and heart-rending candor, have allowed themselves to admit that forbidden hatred and resentment with specific, graphic, intimately personal examples that will surely bring a shock of recognition to all mothers, even those who might desperately insist that they must always love their children "no matter what." Their language is often harsh, perhaps shocking, but their self-revelations manage to evoke the deepest compassion and understanding, which is a tribute to the unique empathy Mr. Lopez displays throughout the book. One inevitably wonders how a male has been able to identify so completely with these female protagonists.

Fortunately, that same empathic insight permeates the seven wives' discussion on the problems of old age.

Having been concerned with the aging process of many of my patients, both men and women, I have read much of the literature on this subject, including Simone de Beauvoir's seminal work, but I have seldom read anything as powerful or as poignantly affective as what I've read in Mr. Lopez's chapter "On Growing Old." I have seen those lonely, timid widows anxiously waiting in the bleak empty lobby of that famous Mexican hotel known as Menopause Manor and their counterparts in the geriatric slums of Miami Beach, the West Side of Manhattan, St. Petersburg, and all the other waiting-to-die sanctuaries that are mentioned with such foreboding by the women in this group. Menopause Manor is a universal nightmare for all of us—for both sexes and for rich and poor alike—but women are taught to look forward to it with horror and shame. They began very early to look for symptoms of middle and old age: "Is this room too warm or am I having hot flashes? . . . Are my breasts sagging more? . . . Are there more crowfeet around my mouth and eyes? . . ." Insistently, fearfully asking those questions, because for a woman "old age" means she is no longer a valuable commodity, no longer sexually attractive, no longer capable of bearing children—and, more often than not, she is unable to contribute financially to the household, much less support herself. Such are the doubts and fears that are expressed with great poignancy in this chapter, and I doubt that anyone can read it without identifying with these women to some degree.

In page after page one is exposed to personal vignettes that won't be easy to forget—a salesman's wife perspiring as she stutteringly explains how she spent the fifty dollars he gave her last week, anxiously accounting for each minimal expenditure she's made and hating him with a near-murderous rage when she sees his lips moving as he inwardly computes each item; the choking anger and shame of a thirty-year-old woman when she reluctantly goes to a precinct station to tell the police she's been raped, listening to the impertinent questions of a grinning cop who obviously thinks that anyone who gets raped "has probably asked for it."

Quite obviously, the emphasis of this book is on the problems of women and how they are trying to find out who they are and what they are capable of doing to develop themselves fully—and of course, many of those problems are faced by men as well. Yet a woman is forced by the very propulsive crush of her rapidly changing environment to reexamine herself in terms of what she had previously accepted or assumed to be her established role, just as these seven wives have painstakingly analyzed their doubts, fears, hopes, and desires, wondering if they can possibly achieve some measure of personal liberation without sacrificing their husbands, their children, and their homes in suburbia.

As a therapist, as a mother, and as a woman I am grateful for this remarkable book, for it sheds a revealing light on one of the central problems of our time, although it raises many troubling questions that will be with us for a long time. But one is inevitably reminded of Gertrude Stein on her deathbed, when Alice Toklas pleadingly asked, "Oh, Gertrude, what is the answer to all this?" and Ms. Stein answering, "Never mind the answer, Alice—what is the question?"

> MILDRED S. LERNER, PhD
> President,
> National Psychological Association
> of Psychoanalysts

Introduction

LAST October, shortly before midnight, I received a long-distance call from an acquaintance of an old friend of mine.

"I want you to help me write a book," he said after identifying himself. "It's a Women's Lib deal. My wife belongs to one of those rap groups that meets every week for what they call consciousness raising."

He didn't have to do much explaining. My wife belongs to a similar group, and I've met at least twenty or thirty women who participate in consciousness-raising sessions.

"Well, anyway," said the gentleman, his voice becoming slightly conspiratorial. "I started getting curious about what they were talking about. They've been meeting at my place—still do—almost every Thursday night, from eight until almost midnight. And my wife asks me to stay away from home on those nights. Stay in town or something. She said my being at home would make the other women, some of them friends of ours, nervous and self-conscious just knowing I was in the house. Even if I stayed completely out of sight in our bedroom upstairs. She mentioned 'negative vibes' or something like that. So you know they've got to be having some pretty heavy conversations. . . ."

Having dutifully stayed away from home on similar nights, I could understand his feeling.

"So," he continued, sounding even more conspiratorial, "I started getting more and more curious about what they were talking about. They could be discussing some pretty intimate things—about sex and other personal stuff. Even my own wife. As a matter of fact, I could see her attitude changing just as soon as those rap sessions started. Her attitude toward me. I mean she was really getting hostile—or else too damned quiet. So I'm naturally curious as hell about those sessions. Seven women talking their ass off every week and not wanting any man around, but nowhere near the house. Well, any guy's got to get awfully fuckin' curious. And finally I couldn't stand it anymore. I had to find out. Somehow. So I got this friend of mine—he's in the electronics business—I got him to bug our living room. That's where they hold these meetings. We did it on her regular shopping day. Pretended I had a bad cold that day and stayed home from the office. So, with all the kids at school, Walter and I had the house all to ourselves. And he had these fantastic little microphones. No wires necessary. Planted them in three spots, hiding them so you'd never know they were there. Then he set up the listening and tape-recording devices behind an old dresser up in the attic, where nobody in the family ever goes.

"Then he set up a timing device, that I could set in the morning before leaving for work so it would start recording at eight P.M. But I had to settle for three-hour tapes. Anyway, to make a long story longer, I've finally recorded sixteen sessions. That's why I'm calling you, Mr. Lopez. Because I'm sure these tapes would make a great book."

"Maybe so," I said. "But I think it's a crappy trick. And besides, it's illegal."

"Not according to my lawyer," he said. "We've discussed it at great length, and he's sure we can avoid litigation by changing all the names, including husbands' occupations, the number and sex of their children, and even setting it in a different locale, yet keeping the essential guts of it."

"How about your wife?" I asked. "She's bound to know it's your deal, even if you call yourself John Doe."

"Never. She'll never know unless I choose to tell her. And I ain't choosing. But you let *me* worry about that. I just want you to help me write this book."

"I don't know," I said. "This sounds pretty hairy to me."

"Well, don't say no, Lopez. Not until we've had a chance to meet each other and let you listen to some of the tapes. Let's discuss this at greater length, go into all the different angles. Then you can decide."

Obviously, I did meet with him and finally realized that he was rather different from what I'd first assumed. As one might expect, his first reaction to the tapes was shock and anger. Then frustration. Finally, it was a long period of despondency. His own wife's statements during the first few sessions had apparently stunned him. He had always assumed their marriage was a fairly happy one. "My God," he told me, "almost all our friends—everyone who met us—kept saying we had a better marriage than most people. So when I heard Mary telling all those women that I was a lousy lay—with all kinds of crappy intimate details—Jesus, man, that hit me like a ton of shit. I couldn't believe it."

Consequently, his first impulse was to leave her, to ask for a divorce. But his lawyer, a most circumspect and philosophical man, persuaded him to wait awhile and to consider his own culpability. "He kept reminding me that I'd been kind of ratty, spying on her that way—that I deserved everything I got."

Later on, after listening to some of the tapes, John's attorney gradually realized that his own consciousness was being raised, that he was learning more about

13

male-female relationships than he had ever known. As a lawyer who had handled many divorces, he had heard hundreds of confessionals from women and men (but mostly women) about to split apart, but none of them had been as revealing as the rap sessions John had recorded.

"Everyone should hear these tapes," he told John. "Especially men. This stuff would blow their minds. Men are never this honest about themselves."

"We can't afford to be," said John. "We can't show our weaknesses this way—not even to our best friends. Certainly not some guy in your own business. You'd be a sitting duck. You've gotta hold your cards pretty close."

"Maybe," said the lawyer. "But we might be better off in other ways."

"I sure as hell wouldn't risk it."

"Well, if I had my druthers, John, I'd make these tapes required listening for every prospective bride and bridegroom in this country. They'd be a lot more important than blood tests."

"Then nobody would get married," said Doe. "I sure wouldn't—not if I knew all this stuff beforehand. Neither would you."

"Maybe. Maybe not. Though I'm not sure anything will prevent people from getting married once they set their minds on it. No matter what they've been told about that holy state."

It was then, after considerable back-and-forth conjecturing, that they decided the secret tapes could provide the basis for an extremely interesting and helpful book. They realized, of course, that all the women's names would have to be changed, occupations of husbands and wives switched around, the number and gender of children altered, everyone's age increased or decreased. "And we'll have to switch the locale from this

14

suburb to another one—perhaps two or three thousand miles away," said the lawyer.

"Why not give it a fictitious name?" John added.

"That's a good idea, John. But all their basic attitudes will remain the same. They'll be no change in essence or emphasis."

"One other thing," said John. "We've got to keep this whole thing to ourselves. You don't discuss this idea with anyone, especially not your wife. I certainly won't let my wife know. She'd probably divorce me—or more likely kill me. And whoever we get to help me write this book, he'll have to make the same pledge."

"So will the publisher," said the lawyer.

"Well, maybe I'll publish it with my own money," Doe suggested. "With all that extra money I've made in the market and those grain futures, I could easily use a tax write-off. So the book doesn't have to make any money. I just want it published. My ego, I guess. Even though I was pretty pissed off when I heard Mary spouting off about our marriage. Now I'm sort of glad I know all those things she's been thinking about me. I guess it could be a helluva lot worse."

Three or four days later John got my home number from an old friend of mine, who will also remain nameless, and called me directly, suggesting an immediate conference. Overcoming my initial skepticism after listening to some of the secret tapes, I was finally persuaded that the recorded rap sessions could indeed provide the basis for a fascinating and valuable book.

The seven wives live in a fashionable suburb which we have renamed Westlake, adjacent to a large city that could easily be Dallas, Los Angeles, Denver, San Francisco, Cleveland, Detroit, Chicago, Boston, New York, Washington, D.C., or Philadelphia. They have met regularly, once a week, mostly at Selma Nathan's house, all the other women providing sandwiches, cookies, and coffee for their ritual midnight snack. Ordinarily, consciousness-raising groups switch their meetings from one participant's house to another's on a rotating basis; but in this particular case, most of the wives felt their husbands would be hostile or derisive, and therefore none of them would be willing to stay away from home whenever they met at "his" house. Thus, as one of the wives asserted during the second session, "We'd never be comfortable at my place. My husband's negative vibes would shoot right through the walls. As a matter of fact, he doesn't know the real purpose of these meetings. I've let him think we're some kind of literature and art group. Other wise, he'd badger the hell out of me."

"So would mine," another one added. "He'd probably try to force me to repeat all the details of what we've been talking about. And I'm sure he'd feel threatened by all this."

Apparently, judging from the tapes we heard, only Selma and Trudy felt confident enough to tell their husbands the real intent of their rap sessions, and both of them had promised not to tell the other husbands.

Their discussions ran the gamut of female concerns, each meeting dealing with a separate topic. They talked about their problems with children, their sexual experiences and attitudes, their money worries, their fear of aging, their ideas on education, job discrimination, *machismo*, male spectator sports, separate vacations, and many other subjects—always with a direct, highly personal frankness that must have been extremely painful and embarrassing for all of them.

Much of that pain is reflected in these fourteen rap sessions. But for the purposes of reader convenience, they have been edited to eliminate repetition, irrelevant references to such things as weather and travel problems, and the usual trivia one would expect in lengthy discussions. Moreover, in order to disguise the real group further, we have altered the original sequence of topics discussed at each meeting.

We hope this book will encourage some of our fellow males to follow the lead of the Seven Wives of Westlake.

E. H. L.

THE SEVEN WIVES OF WESTLAKE

I

Women's Lib in Suburbia

Two women talking often seem to be reciting monologues at each other, neither really listening to (or "judging") what the other is saying. Two personal confessions, two sets of feelings, seem to be paralleling one another, rather "mindlessly," and without "going anywhere." In fact, what the women are doing—or where they are "going"—is toward some kind of emotional resolution and comfort. Each woman comments upon the other's feelings by reflecting them in a very sensitive matching process. The two women share feelings by alternating the retelling of the entire experience in which their feelings are embedded and from which they cannot be "abstracted" or "summarized." Their theme, expressions, pauses, sighs, and seemingly unrelated (or "nonabstract") responses to statements are crucial to such dialogue. A very special prescience is at work here. On its most ordinary level, it affords women a measure of emotional reality and a kind of comfort that they cannot find with men. On its highest level, it constitutes the basic tools of art and psychic awareness.

—PHYLLIS CHESLER,
Women and Madness

"SOME of us may not be acquainted with each other, so perhaps we ought to begin by introducing ourselves. My name is Selma Nathan, and if you'll forgive that sloppy hallway you passed through, welcome to my home. Since most of you feel that your husbands will object to these sessions—or else make fun of them—I guess we'll be meeting here most of the time. Maybe my husband feels the same way, but as a psychoanalyst he'd

21

look pretty silly objecting to something like this. Anyway, these meetings will give Alvin a chance to spend the night away from home. Probably with a young *shiksa* at some motel."

"A young what?" someone asked.

"A *shiksa*—a non-Jewish female—but we'll talk about that later," said Selma. "Let's hear from someone else."

"My name is Rachel Hagler. I guess you might call me a black *shiksa* who's married to a Jewish actor. His name is Jerry."

"I'm Jan Manelli. My husband Ron is in the bowling alley business. We're both Catholics."

"My name is Isabel Phelps. I'm married to a WASP surgeon, so I guess you'd consider me a renegade Jew. My parents certainly do."

"Trudy Steinmetz in this corner. My husband is a tax lawyer. We're both Jewish by birth—agnostics by choice."

"I'm Graciela Ibañez, an ex-Catholic schoolteacher married to Raul who would have been a priest if he hadn't got me pregnant. Actually, he's an executive for Compton-Rex Industries."

"My name is Ruth Kane, a Protestant housewife married to a Protestant surgeon."

"That's a pretty good mix among the husbands," said Selma. "I've counted two doctors, one lawyer, one analyst, two businessmen, and an actor. But we should have had at least one undertaker's wife."

"Or a preacher's," suggested Rachel. "I'd like to see how a preacher's wife would react to one of these consciousness-raising groups."

"She'd probably leave them both—the church and her husband," said Graciela.

"Will it be that bad?" asked Ruth in a slightly

apprehensive voice. "Will this kind of thing actually threaten a marriage?"

"I frankly don't know," said Selma, seeming more serious than before. "Perhaps Anne Lerner can answer that. She's going to be our mediator for one or two sessions. Anne. . . ."

"Well, no one can be sure. Certainly, there's always that possibility—I mean divorce or separation—when a woman takes a good hard look at herself . . . and her marriage. But it could also strengthen a marriage. If it's worth strengthening.

"That's why we've got to talk with each other in the most personal way. It's got to be what *I* feel, what *I* think, what *I* say or said, what *I* do or did. It's always got to be *I*. No one's interested in hearing you tell about someone else. Sometimes, perhaps out of shyness or embarrassment, we all talk about ourselves and our problems as if we're someone else. Like: 'I know this woman who says such-and-such' . . . or 'I have this friend who always so-and-so. . . .' "

General giggling in the background.

"I assume you all know what I'm talking about. But, you see, that's what we've got to avoid in these sessions. We've also got to avoid vague generalities—abstractions. Everything that's said should be as specific as possible. And there's one other rule I should stress: We should never analyze or criticize anyone. We should be supportive rather than analytical. As a matter of fact, you shouldn't analyze your own feelings. Just let yourself go. Let it all hang out. You'll be amazed how easy that is once you get started."

"But what do you mean by *supportive?*" someone asked.

"Just what the word implies," said Anne. "We should support each other—sympathize or, better yet,

23

empathize with the person who's talking. Let her know she's not alone in her fears, her anxieties, her resentments. Not necessarily in words, but in your manner of listening and responding."

"In other words, we shouldn't sit there like some dumb analyst with a blank face," said Rachel, evoking sympathetic laughter. "I had one who sat like a sphinx— never moving a damn muscle or even blinking. I never could figure out what the hell he was thinking."

"I had the same type," said Isabel. "I once tried to crack his mask by telling him I'd like to sleep with him—just to get some response, any kind of response— but he never even smiled. Just sat there with his blank face, making me feel like a silly chippy."

"I'm married to one of those sphinxes"—Selma's throaty, mocking voice. "But don't let that cool mask fool you, sweetie. It's pure defense."

"All right, now," snapped the mediator, obviously wishing to get back on the track, "let's give it a try. Perhaps we should begin with each of you telling us why you're here—what you expect to gain from this experience. Why don't we start with Selma?"

"I'm here because I'm basically unhappy with everything around me—my husband, my children, and mostly myself. For a long time, way before this Women's Lib thing got started, I've had a nagging resentment against my role as a female. First of all, I had to give up my work as a psychologist (and I was a damned good one) to raise my three kids. I kind of accepted what some Libbers call the mother myth. But I'm not so sure it is a myth. We've got to—okay, *I've* got to admit I felt this fantastic sense of creation when those babies were inside me. And that first year or so, watching them develop from one stage to another. That's something no man can experience. Yet it's so damned transitory. And really shitty when you get past that power-of-creation crap.

Especially those lousy smelly diapers and all the mess
kids make. And your husband snoring away like a pig
while you wipe another job of crap off another red fanny.
God, how I hated those soft mushy fannies and that
crying all night long. Then all that boring, boring
housework.

"Worst of all was the god-awful certainty that it
would never be any different, that I was doomed, that I'd
never escape that mother-wife trap. That's when I began
hating Alvin—hated him even while I loved him.
Because he's really more interesting than most men.
Terribly funny and charming when I'm not bitching him
into silence. So I don't want to hate him. I know he's got
his own damned problems as a man, all those weaknesses
and frustrations that I see in my two sons. Yet I keep
wondering if love is possible. I mean *lasting* love. And is it
possible for any woman to be a mother and a wife and
still be herself? I've got to start answering some of these
questions for myself. Perhaps these talk sessions will help
me. I certainly hope so."

"That sort of scares me," said Jan, her voice
quavering slightly. "Because I'm not sure how I feel.
Whether it's hatred or resentment or just plain anger at
myself. All I know is that I sometimes want to scream
and run away . . . run away from everything, from my
children, from my husband, from my house, from everything I know. But mostly, I guess I want to run away
from myself. And like Selma, I'm beginning to feel that
it's all related to my being a woman—and resenting it.
Resenting all the day-to-day crap that's shoved at me
because I am a woman, because I'm a mother and a wife.
But most of all, because I'm a female. If I didn't think
he'd laugh at me—or tell me to go to hell—I'd like to say
these things to my husband. Or to one of my old
girlfriends. But most of them are afraid of this kind of
talk. Maybe I am, too. But I'm going to try."

"I imagine we're all scared," said Rachel in a soft, exploratory tone. "I almost didn't come tonight. I even dialed Selma's number to give some excuse like suddenly getting my period, but her line was busy. Which I took as a sign that I'd better come. I'm mostly afraid that I'll mess my mind worse than it is. Being both black and a woman, I'm not sure what emotional scabs I'll be picking at. A few days ago I read an article about Shirley Chisholm telling someone that she suffered more from being a woman than being black. Well, I'm not so sure about that. Perhaps these talks will help me find out. But if it's racial anger that pours out of me and some of you become the targets, please try to remember that it's not personal. . . ."

"Just let it hang out," urged the mediator as Rachel's voice dissolved to a husky whisper. "Don't worry about anyone else's reaction. It's your consciousness that's got to be raised, and you've got to do most of the raising. . . . Now who's next?"

"Oh! I guess that's me," said Ruth as if she'd been startled from some private musing. "I was just thinking about my husband and what his reaction will be to all this—"

"You're not supposed to tell him," said the mediator. "All that's said here is strictly confidential. You shouldn't tell even your closest female friends what goes on in these discussions."

"Oh, I don't mean that. I'd never tell Walter what we've talked about. Never. I was just wondering what he'll think about my taking off every Thursday night. He's bound to get curious—even suspicious."

"So let him get curious," said Selma. "Let him think you're having an affair with an undertaker."

"But I'm serious, Selma. He'll be awfully curious. I'll have to give him some explanation. I've never done anything like this before."

26

"Of course you will," said Anne. "And it's best to level with your husband. Tell him you're having group discussions with some other women on a regular weekly basis. That it's strictly female talk. But you shouldn't even name anyone in the group."

"That will make him all the more curious. I know how Walter thinks. He'll get downright suspicious."

"So will my husband," Graciela broke in. "But that's his problem. It might do him some good to find something mysterious in me, something he can't know about."

"Well, at least I'm not alone in that respect," said Ruth, her voice still reflecting doubt. "I'm also relieved to know that I'm not the only one who's a little scared about this conscience raising."

"It's our consciousness we're raising," Anne started to explain. "Not our conscience, Ruth. It's a greater awareness of ourselves as women that we're after."

"I'm sorry, Anne. That was just a slip of the tongue. I do see the difference. Though I suppose my conscience will also be raised—or at least nagged. I've always had a nagging conscience, an enormous load of guilt. Especially when I'm unhappy. I feel guilty about the unhappiness— as if it's morally wrong to be dissatisfied. After all, I've got more than most people. I've got a beautiful home, nice clothes, my own car. . . . I suppose it's not being able to produce children that causes most of my guilt. My mother always told me that having children was the most important thing a woman could do. . . . Anyway, I've always been afraid to talk about these things. Or even *think* about them. So that's why I've joined this group. To share my fears with you. Also my hopes."

There was a brief silence and then someone nervously clearing her throat as Graciela began speaking in a clear resonant voice. "I'm no longer afraid. I'm just confused and angry. Ever since I got into Women's Lib

27

about a year ago, I've felt this resentment welling inside me. First I was angry at my husband, and it must have frightened him to see the sudden change in me. Every time I read a new article or book by Kate Millett, Robin Morgan, Gloria Steinem, or anyone else I'd find myself lashing out at Raul as if he represented all men. 'I ought to burn that crap,' he once told me. 'It's poisoning your mind.' He never realized that the poison was already there—that the feminist writers had merely opened a lot of old forgotten wounds. Simply torn the scabs off. Because they'd never really healed. Maybe Raul was right when he said my reading was making me miserable and bitchy—"

"They all say that!" someone shouted.

"But how could I avoid it? Women's Lib was everywhere. In books and newspapers, in all the big magazines, on television talk shows like Dick Cavett and David Suskind. (Although Suskind is always so stupid. I can't stand his attitude, his phony trying to understand.) So, like it or not, we've all been exposed. The cat's out of the bag. Things will never be the same again. Neither will I, nor any of us. And frankly, I don't give a damn if my husband objects to my attending these meetings. I'm not doing it for him—or my marriage. I'm doing this for myself."

"Right on!" yelled several voices.

"I'm with you," agreed Isabel in a flat emphatic manner. "I couldn't care less what my husband thinks about our meetings. I'll be here every Thursday night, no matter what. I'm tired of all the stupid little conventions we've been stuck with—tired of all that good-wife, good-mother nonsense. I want to vomit every time I see one of those TV commercials where mommy's showing daughter what kind of coffee to serve, what kind of floor wax to use, what kind of pills to take so daddy won't see mommy frowning with a headache. My God! how can we ever escape that constant hour-by-hour propaganda on good housekeeping? I'd like to boycott every one of those products."

"Why don't you?"

"Because I need the damn things. Especially the headache pills. Now I still haven't said why I'm here. But I guess my reasons are about the same as all the others we've heard tonight. Except that . . . that I hope this doesn't turn into a wild man-hating binge. I know we'll have to get a lot of resentment out of our systems, but I sure hope it will do something positive. I don't want to hate my husband, I simply want to learn how to like myself as a woman."

"I'm hoping for the same thing," said Trudy, her voice firmer than before. "Though I would add the word 'respect.' I want to like and respect myself. Somehow, during these past few years, I've had less and less respect for myself."

"What do you mean by *respect?*"

"Self-esteem, I guess. I've been losing it day by day. I used to be cocky and sure of myself. I was editor of my college yearbook and a Phi Beta Kappa in my junior year. I had all kinds of boyfriends and two serious proposals before graduation. But instead of getting married, I got a job as an assistant producer at CBS. Then I got hitched to an alcoholic writer, whom I wisely divorced two years later. Still working but feeling slightly shaken, I looked around for the safest kind of man I could find. Security was the watchword—psychological, as well as financial. So what could be more secure than a successful young lawyer associated with a large law firm? But that's when my ego started to crumble. Right from the beginning (our first date, in fact) he regarded me as a very charming and sexy nitwit who needed protection, and I fell right into that stupid role. . . ."

"Oh-oh, I can see it coming," someone said, apparently unable to resist comment.

"And you're dead right," agreed Trudy. "Anyone could have seen it coming. Except me. It seems so easy, so relaxing, to drift into that Dumb Dora state. No need to compete anymore against my apprehensive cutthroat male colleagues in that television rat race. I'd play tennis instead. And read all those heavy novels I'd been buying but never reading. Dumb Dora, the sneak reader. But the strain of acting dumb—I mean charmingly dumb—was harder than earning my Phi Beta Kappa key. Though after a while the strain was less and less as I got dumber and dumber. Genuinely dumb. Then when Ronnie was born, with all his neurological problems, I became numb most of the time. Numb and dumb. And that's where I am now. Except that I know damned well I'm *not* dumb. And I'm determined to shake myself free of the numbness. I also want to get rid of all the self-pity that's been burying me under."

"You've made a pretty good start," said the mediator when Trudy had finished. "I think you've all made a good beginning. But I think we ought to adjourn fairly soon. These opening sessions are a heavy psychic drain, particularly for first timers."

"May we ask a few questions before we call it a night?"

"Sure. But let's not get too involved."

"Well, first of all," asked Rachel, "could you tell me if my emotions will settle down between meetings? Or will they stay at the same high pitch I'm feeling now?"

"Not likely," said Anne. "But you're bound to have highs and lows, and your general emotional state will be a bit more agitated than before. Your husbands will no doubt comment upon that fact."

"So we can expect a lot of static at home?"

"Probably. But a lot of that static will come from

you. Your husbands and kids will simply be reacting to the radical change in you."

"Radical?"

"I should hope so," said the mediator. "That's what this is all about. We're after basic changes in our attitudes about ourselves. Only then can we hope to change—and I mean *fundamentally* change—the society that's made us what we are."

"That's a pretty big order."

"It sure is. . . ."

"Anne?"

"Yes, Jan."

"I'm just wondering how the kids will react to all this?"

"Well, they'll probably think you've suddenly gotten pretty bitchy and hard to live with."

"I'm already bitchy," observed Selma offhandedly. "I've been that way a long time. My daughter Shari calls me a bitch every time we argue—three or four times a week—"

"Mine, too," someone interjected as Selma continued:

"But the boys are more respectful. They hardly ever call me bitch. Except when I'm bitchier than usual. So one more degree of bitchiness will hardly be noticed."

"You're lucky," said Jan. "I mean that your kids are used to it. I'm afraid mine will be sorta shocked when I let go. I've always tried to put on this damned good-mommy image. Hardly any cussing. Just a few damns now and then."

"Don't worry about that," said Rachel. "They've heard it from other kids' mommies."

"Well, it's not really the language that worries me. It's having to be bitchy, outwardly bitchy. I've always saved that for my husband. Now my kids will be in the line of fire."

31

"But why should you spare them?" asked the mediator. "They'll have to learn some time. So why shouldn't they learn right now—from you if no one else—what it's like to be a woman? . . . Your daughters, if you have any, should particularly find out how you really feel as a woman . . . and especially as a wife."

"I wish to hell my mother had shown me," said Selma, deep irony in her husky voice. "All she ever told me was how to push up my little boobies so I could attract a nice Jewish doctor."

There was a burst of laughter, then several remarks about mothers crisscrossing each other until the mediator's commanding voice cut through the chatter. "Now that's a good subject for a future meeting—what our mothers told us about being a woman. But I think your next session should deal with sex and marriage."

"That's a good idea," said Selma. "Now let's have a final cup of coffee and some cheesecake that my mother taught me how to make. So, you see, it wasn't a total loss. God bless that sweet, suffering *nebech*."

II

Children

Most children in contemporary American culture invade their mother's privacy, life space, sanity and selves to such an extent that she must give up those things in order not to commit violence.

—PHYLLIS CHESLER,
Women and Madness

ISABEL began the second session with a flat, blunt statement that apparently startled some of the group.

"To be perfectly frank," she said, "I hate all my kids. I guess I've always hated them—except for the first nine months, when they were like little dolls and couldn't cause much trouble."

"I can't believe that," said Trudy.

"Believe what?"

"That you've always hated them—not really."

"Listen, Trudy—" Resentment flaring in Isabel's flat voice. "We're supposed to level with each other, and I'm just telling you how I really feel about my kids. I know damned well I'm not supposed to hate them or even resent them. But there's no sense kidding myself. I've even seen a couple of psychologists about my feelings, and right away they start bugging me about my sex life, as if *that* has anything to do with how I feel about those darned kids. I mean really, now. Why must it always get down to sex whenever you see a shrink?"

33

"Maybe it does—" someone started to say.

But Isabel ignored any interruptions and plunged ahead. "I told both those shrinks that I really loved Linda and Little Chris when they were first born, especially Linda. She was really adorable that first year. Cuddly and sweet, always smiling and gurgling as if she couldn't keep all that happiness inside. Just gurgling all the time. And I used to gurgle with her—did it all the time, just the way she gurgled—until Big Chris told me I was acting like a damned fool. He couldn't stand the way we loved each other, couldn't bear to be left out. So he started telling me she'd never learn to talk if I kept on gurgling the way she did. But that wasn't his real reason. He was jealous, that's all. He couldn't stand that closeness between Linda and me. Men never do. Anyway, he kept bugging me about it till I finally couldn't stand hearing him anymore. Then I went into a different stage with her after that. I didn't gurgle or say much of anything to her—just let her make noises to herself. . . ."

"That's too bad," someone whispered.

"But then Linda started saying a few words. I guess she got them from the baby-sitter, this college girl who lived down the street and took care of her whenever we went out, which was pretty often. And, for some darned reason, I guess I resented that—I mean the way Linda started to learn all these new words from someone else."

"You obviously wanted her to remain a baby," Graciela broke in. "That's why you used all that baby talk, that gurgling bit. I remember that from my psych course at UCLA. You were—"

"Hey there! You're analyzing," said Selma. We're not supposed to do that. We're supposed to be supportive, not analytical."

"But I *was* being supportive, Selma. I just wanted her to know the reasons—the psychological reasons—for all that gurgling bit, and letting the baby-sitter. . . ."

"That's still analyzing, sweetie."

"Will both of you shut up!" snapped Isabel, her voice rising to a higher level of flatness. "I haven't made my point yet—about when I started hating her that way. I guess it started when Linda began talking. Jabbering really. Jabber, jabber, jabber, all day long. And the worst part was after that baby-sitter (Gwen Something-orother) taught her to say 'potty.' So it was potty this and potty that. Every damned thing she touched or saw was POTTY. She even called me Potty. . . ." 1771580

Repressed laughter from someone.

"But not Big Chris, mind you. Oh, no. He was always *daddy*—plain as she could say it—daddy. Well, it happened that way with every new word she learned. She kept repeating and repeating it until I was ready to strangle her, ready to go out of my mind. And somehow she seemed to sense my anger and frustration. She actually seemed to be taunting me. She really did. Especially with that potty routine. For two or three weeks that's all I heard from her—potty, potty, potty, potty, potty, potty, potty—till I was practically climbing the walls. So then I'd put on the damned radio loud as I could. Mostly that horrible rock-and-roll music I can't stand. God, she was bitchy. I mean really bitchy. . . ."

There was a long silence.

"Then along came Little Chris," she said finally. "He was so darned cute and cuddly I didn't seem to mind Linda anymore. We had a different baby-sitter for him—one of those grandmotherly types you hardly find these days. But this time *I* decided to teach him how to talk. I'd point to my nose and say 'nose,' then my mouth and my eyes, or maybe a chair or a table. But he wouldn't say a word, not a single damn word. He'd get this silly grin on his face, pointing at something but not saying anything except for this funny noise that sounded

like *glub*. For two whole years—maybe it was three—
that's all he could say: glub, glub, glub. I honestly
thought he would never learn to talk, and Big Chris got
all uptight and even started blaming *me*, accusing me of
screwing the kid's mind with baby talk, and here I was
knocking myself out all day long, trying to teach him just
any damn word. I even tried *pottty!* Though it made me
constipated to think about that horrible word. So there I
was, listening to Linda jabbering away like an idiot
auctioneer and Little Chris mumbling his *glub glub glub*
all day long, the whole damned day, from early morning
till bedtime. And all the damned trouble they got into,
breaking this and dirtying that and never, never letting
me rest—not one single damned moment of peace that I
can remember. Jesus, how I waited and prayed for them
to go to sleep. But by then *he* would be home. Big Chris.
The original gripe, fussing about this and moaning about
that and guzzling so much scotch I often wondered how
he ever got sober enough to operate on anybody the next
morning."

"He was a surgeon?"

"That's what he was, Grace, a gastrointestinal
surgeon, and I'd hate to see some of the guts he
scrambled during one of those hangovers. But I guess I
had a few myself—I mean the hangovers. Because
sometimes I tried to match him drink for drink as he sat
there bitching about my housework and not being able to
keep the damned kids quiet when he got home. Jesus!
Here I'd been listening to them for twelve hours, twelve
earsplitting hours, and he couldn't stand them for one
measly half hour. I wanted to choke him when he said
those things, I really did. And I kept wondering if he had
any idea what it was to spend all your living days trying
to raise a couple of wild animals. Because that's all they
were to me, a couple of animals, and I kept feeling so
awful damned guilty 'cause I couldn't bring myself to

love them, really love them, the way a mother's supposed
to. And I wonder if any man can ever understand that
kind of mother hate. And yet I know that I've always
loved them. Somewhere in my lonely sick heart I must
have loved them even while I was hating them."

"Of course you did," said Selma after a long pause.
"I'm all choked up when I hear you say those things,
Isabel, and it's because I've so often felt that way myself.
I guess it's natural to resent—and finally to hate—anyone or anything that robs you and cheats you out of your
own life. That's our whole problem. Having to give so
much of ourselves day after day after day, including
weekends. Probably worse on weekends, because then
we've got the biggest babies of all to look after. Our lousy
damned husbands."

"Right on!" said several voices.

"But getting back to the kids," Selma continued. "I
can certainly understand how you feel, Isabel. It's truly a
never-ending job when you've got little kids. My little
Jerry was a hellcat from the minute he started to crawl. I
couldn't turn my eyes away for a single minute. He was
everywhere. Into the toilet bowls, under the stairs, out to
the patio when anybody left the door open, and he once
crawled into the damned clothes dryer. I could have
slapped the door shut without knowing he was there, for
God's sake. And maybe I should have. That's how I felt
sometimes. I just wanted to be rid of him. Especially
when he started talking and asking all those goddamned
questions, millions and millions of questions about every
damned thing under the sun."

"But that was great!" exclaimed Trudy. "He was
exercising his brain, he was—"

"There you go, Trudy. Analyzing again. We're not
into that bag, sweetie."

"Sorry, Selma. I guess it's my psychology background. I keep forgetting."

"Well, anyway, I got sick of all his questions and his nosing around everywhere. I once dreamed—and it was a daydream, mind you—that Jerry had crawled back into my womb and turned back into a fetus and kept getting smaller and smaller and smaller until he became a dinky little sperm again. Nothing but a sperm again. So then all I had to do was take a big fat douche and flush him out."

"That's awful," said someone indistinctly.

"*Oi vey*," said Selma with a sigh in her voice. "We've got one of those Catholics among us. So now I'm not even permitted a retroactive contraception."

"Except that I'm a Protestant," said Ruth, her voice now easily identified. "One of those full-fledged WASP's that Mailer is always sneering at. And you misunderstood my remark. It wasn't meant to be critical and certainly nothing against birth control. I guess it was more envy than anything. Because, you see, I've never been able to have a child. So getting rid of one—even so indirectly as what you call *retroactive contraception*—makes me feel sort of like a starved beggar watching a fat millionaire throwing away good food. Or maybe vomiting it."

"Them's pretty harsh words," said Selma. "But I guess I asked for it. Though I didn't mean to be flip. Not at all. I really did dream about his crawling back into my womb and all the rest of it. Sort of killing him the easy way, I guess. And Alvin got it worse. That's my husband. I've gotten rid of him in my dreams a dozen ways, mostly by accidental drowning, maybe once a month for the last sixteen years. He's replaced my mother, God bless her ever-loving soul. But it's a funny thing about my daydreams. I don't remember ever getting rid of my other two kids, Shari and little Sid. Of course they never asked as many questions as Jerry did—or maybe Jerry answered them when I wasn't around. So they didn't bug me as much. Except that Shari got to be quite a little bitch even before she was ten. She had the foulest mouth I ever heard on a kid, boy or girl. Some she got from her two older brothers and a cousin who came to visit one summer. But most of her really foul language—shit and fuck and all the rest of it—she probably got from Alvin, this let-em-be-free husband of mine. Alvin the analyst, who thinks any rule or inhibition is already a crime against nature. . . ."

Long pause, then Selma again.

"That's a funny thing about the word 'analyst.' In one of our earlier sessions I realized that the first four letters spell *anal,* and there's nobody more anal than Alvin. Especially when he talks. So from him our little Shari gets all the four-letter words you'd be ashamed to hear from a boy or any teen-ager. Even Portnoy would be shocked by Shari at the age of ten. But not her daddy. To him it's all cute and liberated. Not only that—he also knows it sickens me to hear her. So that's also a plus in his eyes. Papa and daughter talking like a couple of who-knows-what, and Shari getting so there's no controlling her once she gets into junior high, where she's obviously got to become the leading sexpot of north Westlake and all points east and west. Never mind when she gets really sexy with her little boobs crowding her sweaters like oversized oranges. Then it's the whole bunch of them giving me headaches, not to say heartaches, when Jerry and Sid and even Shari get into the pot scene at school. And who knows how many of those kids are into drugs? Probably all their friends and maybe some of the teachers, because you can't know about them either."

"I guess it's everywhere," said Rachel. "Certainly with my two kids. They tried to hide it with incense, but you can always tell."

"Linda's also been fooling around with it."

"So have my kids—at least two of them. Joe and Billie and maybe Frank. But if my husband ever catches them, I'd hate to see what happens. I guess Ron would almost kill them. He's really hard on the drug business. He'd certainly want to kill the pusher if someone got Mary hooked on pot or pills or anything else. That would really. . . . Well, I really can't say what he'd do. Something pretty awful."

"Well, maybe he's right," said Graciela. "We've got to start fighting this somewhere down the line. Though I'm not especially worried about pot. I've tried it myself a couple of times, I mean without Raul knowing about it. He's gotten so square I wouldn't dare tell him about my smoking pot. So you can imagine what he would do to Jose and Erlinda, especially the girl. He'd probably call her a whore."

"They don't get along?"

"Well, right now they do. She's only twelve, and she's got him wrapped but completely wrapped around her little finger. And we all know about that sort of thing. Favorite spoiled daughter—until she gets into something like drugs, which (thank God or I hope to God) she hasn't."

"What do you think he'd do, Graciela?" someone asked in a soft, tentative voice.

"Gee, it's hard to say about Raul. He's sometimes a total mystery to me. But I do know he resents my attitude about her."

"About whom?"

"About Erlinda. He's convinced that I hate her, that I'm jealous of her, that I'm always trying to pick on her. The slightest criticism from me will—will—will make him blow up. Just like that. And she's taking full advantage of it. Grates on my nerves with all kinds of ploys and devious mean little—mean little—I mean all kinds of nasty remarks. And never doing anything around the house, except make a peanut butter and jelly sandwich now and then, without ever—not once— putting the jars and bread away, but leaving everything there on the kitchen table, with the damned jelly knife smearing everything. Then calling me a bitch under her breath, but loud enough for me to hear, when I yell at her to clean up her own messes. And there's Raul. . . ."

"Raul what?"

"Sitting there with the afternoon paper or just staring at the TV and yelling for me to shut up. Telling *me* to shut up, but never saying a thing to *her*—never, I mean never, never, never. . . ."

The rising pitch of her voice was suddenly cut short by general laughter, the laughter of sudden recognition.

"That's my house," said Jan. "You've been describing almost exactly what happens at my place every day. Especially the peanut butter and jelly."

"And the damned knives," added Selma. "Alvin yelling his ass off and asking for peace and Shari smearing *three* knives—one with jelly, one with peanut butter, one with plain butter—and all of them left on the kitchen table while little Miss America goes back to her bedroom to stare at the soap operas like a damned zombie as she stuffs her daddy-sweet mouth with calories, which will make her a regular fat Jewish mama before she's even married. And the Prince of Peace, our favorite anal analyst, yelling for *peace in this house!* And me whispering to Shari, 'COME BACK AND CLEAN THIS UP, YOU LITTLE BITCH!' Because now I've learned their language. But never *shit*, mind you, 'cause that kind of anal talk I won't stoop to. Regardless of provocation."

Again general laughter and high-pitched giggling, some of it from Selma herself. Then Rachel in a suddenly solemn voice.

"At least we can laugh about all that messiness in

the kitchen, and sometimes even the pot scene can be a little funny. But I've got myself some problems that get me down, really down. Both of my kids have got to deal with the color problem, especially Ben. He's my child by my first husband—who was also black, blacker than me. And Jean is my girl from this second marriage with Jerry, who's white. You remember my telling you he's an actor."

"Would that be Jerry Hagler?"

"The very same. And Jean's almost as light as he is. So people sometimes don't realize she's part black. She could easily pass, though that's the last thing she'd want to do. She's even got a big afro wig like Angela Davis, and that cut-off hair underneath is as straight and silky as yours, Ruthie."

"I've seen her at the bus stop, Rachel. She's lovely. Just like a high-fashion model."

"That's what her daddy says. But my son Ben is a bit different, a lot different. He's pretty dark. There's no mistaking what he is. And of course he's proud of that. Yet I sometimes get the feeling that he's about bust out of his skin, as if he's got something boiling inside that's about to explode. He won't talk about it—with anyone, I guess—but I'm sure it all started when he got to senior high school and all this dating thing got serious. It's no longer that everyone's-in-the-gang business that gets you through junior high when you're the only black kid in school. Jean is there, of course, but Ben is the only kid at Horace Mann who's really black."

"I don't understand, Rachel. I've seen several, maybe twenty, black kids at the high school."

"Yes, but most of them (except for Doreen Berry in the tenth grade) are fairly light-skinned Negroes, the kind we call high yaller, Selma. But Ben's really dark, and his features are more African. So he's bound to have more problems with the white girls than some of the

42

other black kids. Now, I'm not saying none of them will date him. One or two *have* dated him."

"How about the other black girls at school?"

"Well, I guess some of them have their own hangups on color. They seem to prefer the blacks with the lighter skin—or some of the white kids. That's old stuff with some of us. Look at me, for example. . . . Benjie must think about that, too, when he's thinking about girls and wondering why his own mother married white the second time around."

"Maybe that's why he won't talk to you about the girl business," suggested Jan.

"Now that's analyzing again," protested Selma.

"That's okay. I don't mind," said Rachel. "I've been asking myself the same sort of questions. Racking my brain for some new angle, some sort of miracle solution to this whole color problem. Worrying and worrying about Ben and sometimes wishing I were married to a black man again and living somewhere where blacks are in the majority, where he could have his choice of lots of girls his own color. Then he wouldn't be worried about sudden rejection or some white liberal gal dating him out of pity or curiosity or just to bug her parents—and never, never really knowing what's below the surface. That question is always there, you know. I've seen it in Ben's eyes, in the tight quiver of his lip, but mostly in his eyes, when he's dated or even talked for a long while with some white girl at school or at that hamburger joint where the kids hang out. It nearly kills me to see that tentative, uncertain look in his face and then listening to his voice get just a little louder to mask that feeling of not knowing what all these white people are really thinking, and suddenly feeling acutely aware of yourself, of your skin and your hair and maybe your lips. We've got this damned perpetual mirror all around us, never letting us forget who we are and what we look like to others."

"But you're beautiful, Rachel."

"Of course, we are, Trudy. But we've been psyched and brainwashed by white folks' standards for so many years, so many *centuries,* that some of us can't always know that black *is* beautiful. I myself know at least five or six black men—two of them big actors like Jerry—who simply can't have sex with a black woman. Can't get it up. No matter how hard they try. And certain black women are hung up the same way, though thank God I'm not one of them. I've had myself a black husband and bore him a child, a beautiful child. Yet I'm frankly so screwed up about this color thing. I'm so damned ambivalent in my deep-under feelings, that I'm a living version of *Ebony* magazine, preaching black-is-beautiful in some article and right on the next page a big fancy picture ad telling black women how to straighten their nappy hair and lighten their skin with this cream and that cream, and those skinny models with white people's noses and long-haired wigs—all of it giving us a whole different message on the Afro bit. No wonder our minds are so scrambled. . . ."

Long, long silence, as if no one knows how to respond—then Rachel's voice again.

"So if I can't tell where I'm at or where I'm coming from, how can I possibly expect poor Ben to get himself together? He's got to be hurting most of the time, hurting and getting angrier all the time and maybe getting ready to explode someday. I guess that's why he's been drinking all that wine lately—wine and pot and all that loud funky music."

"They're all doing it, Rachel. I can smell the stench of it—along with beer—in Jerry's room almost every weekend."

"But not the way Ben does it. All the other kids do it in gangs or at least with a couple of friends. Ben drinks all alone. And plays the same record over and over again.

Then he'll get in his car and drive off like a blind fool, racing off like he can't wait to get nowhere."

"How about his sister? Can she reach him?"

"Well, sometimes they talk. But mostly they argue and get on each other's nerves. She's at that difficult age—just over fourteen—and Ben's almost seventeen. So there's not much there, by way of communication, I mean. And I guess he sort of resents all those kids she hangs around with. It's a mixed crowd, but mostly white. She's lighter, you see. And her hair's soft and straight. . . ."

"How about your husband and Ben?"

"Well, Jerry's always trying. But it's a real strain. You can see it right away. Jerry doing most of the talking and Ben answering as little as possible. Just enough to be polite and never volunteering anything on his own. They were much closer when Benny was a child, when we were first married. Then things began to change when Ben was around ten or eleven. That black-white mess started creeping in. Not anything dramatic, mind you. Nothing I can even remember at this time. Just one little thing after another, most of it coming from outside but having an impact inside. So no matter how hard Jerry tried on the inside (at home), he couldn't cope with all that outside stuff that started bugging Benny, mostly at school and on the playground down the street or maybe some other kid's house. People making him feel like a nigger everywhere he'd go, and finally Jerry getting all the resentment pouring out at home. Silent resentment. The worse kind, I guess. . . . Now, I'm not going to say anymore. I'm hogging this show."

"Don't worry about that, Rachel. It's got to come out. You'll get plenty from us," said Selma soothingly. "And you're also teaching us a lot."

"Well, I've had my say for now."

"Okay then. I guess Trudy's next."

There was a muffled noise before Trudy began, perhaps the scraping of a chair on the carpet. Then a soft hesitant voice that came in and out of focus.

"I don't know where to begin, except that I'm feeling a little less sorry for myself than when we first started. I've also resented my son from time to time and maybe hated him. Yet I've never wanted to think of myself that way. I certainly wouldn't have admitted any sort of hate against Ronnie, not even to myself. Then I heard all of you tonight having the courage to say it out loud and really admitting what you feel about children. It's sort of comforting in a funny—well, not really funny, but in a strange kind of way. To know that you're not alone in resenting someone you're always supposed to love, especially a child. But I still can't help feeling guilty, horribly guilty, when I feel any kind of resentment toward Ronnie. So it's even hard to *think* about hating him or wanting to be rid of him. Because he can't help himself. He was born the way he is. He suffers from dyslalia and dyslexia, both due to brain damage before he came out of the womb. So it was really my fault or his father's fault—or both of us. Some sort of punishment from God, I guess. How, how else—how else can you explain something like that?"

Her voice had cracked and faded to a bare whisper, someone apparently sobbing on the far side of the room.

"But, Trudy darling, it wasn't your fault. You can't go on blaming yourself."

"Such things happen—with nobody to blame," someone added.

"But they were my genes. And also John's. The defect was in us. So now Ronnie has to suffer for it. All the rest of his life. Not being able to read like everyone else. His vision so distorted that I must look like a monster to him. And he can't control his body movements either because of the dyslalia."

46

"What's that?" asked Jan.

"Well, it's some kind of brain damage. I've got the medical definition stuck in my mind, word for word. 'Dyslalia is a defect in articulative power caused by a malfunction or imperfect distribution of nerves to the organs of articulation.' But they're just words to me, words I can't really understand. The doctors have tried to explain it to me, with pictures and drawings, but I keep blanking out when they're telling me. It's too complex. All I know is that Ronnie's a lot different from other kids, that he can't care for himself, that I've got to be there most of the time, trying to teach him how to read letter by letter the way the therapists have showed me and wanting to cry all the time knowing how helpless and frustrated—and cheated—he must feel. Because he *does* feel and he *does* think. The doctors say he may have an average or more-than-average intelligence, that he's thinking all the time, but without being able to express it. And I keep groping for that intelligence, trying, trying, trying to pull it out of him. But, you see, I can't. . . . I can't. . . ."

Someone coughed, then cleared her throat. And after a long pause, Trudy went on.

"Some of you mentioned getting rid of your kids. In your dreams, I mean. Well, that's happened to me, too. Except that I'm always with Ronnie. In one of my dreams we're hit by a huge truck as we're crossing a street. In another one we drown together with no one there. In another dream, the one that comes most often, we simply disappear into nowhere. Just like that. But he never disappears alone. I'm always with him. . . . And I guess John would like it that way. He could be rid of both of us. He'd be free again. He wouldn't have to come home anymore to listen to my complaints and my worries and all my pent-up anger. But at least he doesn't have to deal with Ronnie. Most of the time he comes home after

Ronnie's asleep. As a matter of fact, I think he works late on purpose. So he won't have to see him and feel guilty. He's shut Ronnie out of his life completely—seldom mentions the kid's name anymore and never seems to listen when I'm talking about Ronnie.

"Consequently, Ronnie's *my* problem, mine alone. But God, how it wears me out. By the time John gets home I'm completely worn out, ready to cave in, or else I'm all nerves. Jittery and frustrated and spitting angry. One word from John, one nasty crack or even a grunt, and I'm ready to scream or scratch his goddamned eyes out. Just anything to release that awful tension and anger. And it frightens me so, it really scares me—to know that I can hate that much, that I'm ready to kill someone. . . . Yes, even Ronnie. And that's the worse part. To feel that kind of hate from a mother. But when I listen to all of you, when I know someone else can feel that way about their kids, then I know I'm not alone. That it isn't just me, that maybe you don't have to be insane to resent your own child."

"Of course you don't," said Selma in a husky, half whisper. "Because if you do, then we've got a country full of mad females. Almost every woman I've ever talked to has felt that way at one time or another."

"How about you, Jan?" asked Graciela. "I've seen you shaking your head now and then, but not saying anything."

"Well, I guess I'm a little different, Grace. I've got five kids, four boys and a girl spaced two years apart, and I've hated them all from time to time. But I can't honestly remember ever wanting to kill any of them or wanting to get rid of them in some dream. My husband, yes. I've even gone so far as to tell Ron to his face that I'd like to kill him. That's why he doesn't carry life insurance. He probably believes me." She laughs with the others. "Maybe he should. I mean I'm dead serious when I tell him those things. But not my kids. I could never say it to them—Jesus, no. I think I'd drop dead for even thinking that way. I couldn't face my priest. How could I tell him, 'Father, I've been thinking of killing Larry or Billie. . . .' I couldn't do it. So what I can't confess I can't dream."

"You're kidding, Jan."

"Kidding about what?"

"That you've never dreamed about something you didn't confess afterward."

"Well, maybe not. I mean maybe so. There's been some sex I didn't bother to mention to Father Angelo."

"Actual sex or dream sex?"

"Well, the actual sex I'd have to mention. But the dreams I figured were no harm to anyone. So those I've never confessed. I had quite a few dreams about this plumber who came when the upstairs john kept flooding over. We didn't actually do anything—just some fast hot necking and rubbing in the hallway. But, Jesus, I kept dreaming about him almost every night for about a month. And the funny thing about it, his name was Joe—like my older boy, who's seventeen. That plumber couldn't have been more than twenty-six. So for a while there I couldn't call Joe by his real name 'cause it made me feel kind of guilty, you see. I started calling him Sonny, till he reminded me that his name was Joe. Who wants to be called Sonny if he already knows he's your son and his name is Joe? But all of that, the dreams and everything, I never bothered to confess to Father Angelo.

"Once, however, I told him how much I hated little Mary. She's next to the youngest, about eleven years old and a real brat. If it was only peanut butter and jelly sandwiches and a sloppy bedroom, that wouldn't be so bad. You expect that. I was like that myself. Yet there's something awfully nasty about that girl, something I can't understand. She's always lying and stealing and pulling these dirty little deals on her own friends. I hear her on the phone, plotting this and plotting that. Lying, deliberately lying, to this friend to get her mad at another one. Then calling the other one, the one she's lied about, and crisscrossing the lies—all the time pretending this goddamned innocence. And they're not just little fibs, harmless little-girl fibs. They're nasty and mean. So I finally had a big session with her, one of those mother-daughter sessions, about three months ago. Well, she denied everything. She started accusing *me*. She sat there and accused me of inventing lies because I hated her. She started bawling and screaming and threatening to run away. Then when daddy got home, she gave him the big crying scene, finally telling him, 'I think mommy's sick.' And that bastard sat there and took all that shit! I mean he really took it in.

"Finally, it was Joe and Billie who took up for me. They had to tell him that Mary had it coming, that she was doing exactly what I said she'd done. But I could see that both of them were really more interested in establishing some kind of temporary truce between us. They just wanted a little peace around the house. They're awfully nice kids—all my boys are. Not goody-goody, mind you. Joe and Billie have their share of the pot scene and the drinking we talked about earlier. He's even had a sex problem with this girl he's running around with. But by and large, none of them give me half the problems I get from little Mary."

"Has Father Angelo talked to her, Jan?"

"You mean Mary?"

"Right. I was thinking he—"

"I've asked him to—about two months ago. But I think she conned him. She must have put on that daddy's-little-girl trick that will con any man alive. You can't imagine such hurt innocence. She's a regular Shirley Temple with bangs when any male's around,

including priests. So what happens? the very next time I
see Father Angelo, a week or so later, he's giving me one
of those heart-to-heart talks about parental tolerance—
how mothers have to take special pains with daughters.
He'd apparently talked with Ron in the meantime and
finally concluded that I'm the one mostly to blame."

"Isn't that typical?" said Isabel. "We're always to
blame. It's always the mothers."

"But what can you expect from a priest?" asked
Graciela. "The church would always take that stand.
Husbands have no responsibility for kids. Mama does—
and then gets all the damned blame. So don't go
expecting a Catholic priest to see it your way. He's got a
Holy Virgin complex up to his ears, and unless you're as
spotless as *she* is, Jan, you've got problems. That's why
you don't dare tell him about screwing that plumber in
your dreams—"

"You're analyzing, Grace," protested Selma. "We're
not supposed to do that."

"Because you know damn well that priest would
probably consider it as bad as the real thing—which
maybe it is, according to dogma. But he'd only say
tch-tch of your husband's dreaming that way. Male sins
don't mean as much to those priests. It's the *women* they
want to remain virgins. That's their whole worry about
legalizing abortions. It might mean more sex for us, and
sex is dirty. Sex means no more virgins. No more of that
Holy Virgin crap. . . ."

"But, Graciela," said Ruth, breaking in, "aren't you
also a Catholic?"

"Not really, not anymore. I'm sick of that reactionary church. I swallowed all that stuff for years. I kept
going to mass way after I stopped believing, because I
thought it was good for my kids and because I'm still
hung up on the esthetic part of it—the incense, the choir
singing, the beautiful altars, and stained-glass windows,

51

all those things that make Catholicism so appealing. Not all the reactionary business. Well, I'm happy to say that Jose and Erlinda don't go for any of it. They never go to church. Even when Raul tries to force them. So he goes alone. Without any of us."

"Same with my kids," said Selma. "They never set foot in a synagogue. Except for one special occasion, the boys' bar mitzvahs. Also during the Six-Day War, but that was mostly a patriotic thing."

"Ben and Jean never go to any church," said Rachel. "None of us do. We're not into religion of any kind."

"Linda goes," said Isabel. "She goes with her daddy, while Little Chris and I stay home and eat huge Sunday breakfasts and listen to his music, mostly rock."

"Our whole family goes," said Jan. "To ten o'clock mass every Sunday and holiday. Only sickness is an excuse. Then it's always a big brunch at Howard Johnson's. Sometimes I'd like to stay home and sleep real late, maybe till midafternoon. Just by myself. But Ron would never stand for that. He'd drag me out of bed."

"Why don't you try it someday?" asked Grace.

"Maybe I will. But I think I'd have to get drunk first. Three Bloody Marys would do it. Maybe four."

"That's a fair exchange," said Grace.

"What?" asked Jan.

"Four Bloody Marys for one Virgin Mary."

"That's awful!" exclaimed Ruth. "That's an awful way to talk!"

"Not when you're a Catholic," said Jan. "Especially if you're a fallen Catholic. I guess we're the most profane people you'll ever meet. My dad was always making cracks like that."

III

On Growing Old

. . . but old age is the general fate, and when it seizes upon our own personal life we are dumbfounded. . . .

—SIMONE DE BEAUVOIR,
The Coming of Age

SELMA began the meeting with an announcement concerning another member of the group.

"That was Ruth on the phone. She's not coming tonight. She just told me she'd gotten halfway to my house, then suddenly made a U-turn and went back home again. She said, 'I have such a hard time even *thinking* about getting old that I don't think I could stand talking about it.' So we'll have to go on without Ruthie's contribution to our discussion."

"She's already made it," said Rachel. "She's told us how she feels in the most graphic way she could. And, quite frankly, I almost stayed away myself. But I didn't have enough courage to be an honest coward."

"I felt the same way," admitted Isabel, chuckling at Rachel's comment. "Then I finally said 'to hell with it—if I'm old I'm old—no sense avoiding.' So here I am."

"You can easily say that," said Trudy. "Because you don't look anywhere near your age, Isabel. Certainly not forty-three."

"That's just my face, sweetie. Plastic surgery about a

53

year ago. But look at my hands and wrists. I feel like a spook."

"I'd settle for that," responded Trudy. "I'd love to get rid of these horrible bags, but with all Ronnie's medical bills, we couldn't afford it right now. Nevertheless, I keep. . . ."

Her voice faltered as Selma broke in with a question. "Anyone else have plastic surgery—I mean aside from a nose bob like mine?"

"I almost did," said Rachel. "Just before I quit my acting career. But my husband talked me out of it—the cheapskate. Said it would take all the character out of my face."

"Maybe, it's just as well." Isabel sighed, her usual flat monotone sagging at the end of each phrase. "You can fix the outside for a while, but the inside keeps getting old fast as ever."

(The silence that followed was so prolonged I thought the tape had snagged in the recorder. Then a timid question came from Jan.)

"Was the surgery painful, Isabel?"

"Painful as hell. Your face feels and looks as if a bunch of wildcats have torn it apart. Then you have this long, long wait, wondering if the damned operation was successful. You have to go into seclusion for several months so your friends won't see you. There you sit, alone and embarrassed, needing company more than ever but too ashamed to face anyone. It's like being exiled in your own home—which is the worst part of it—being shut away in your own house, where everything around you is a reminder of the miserable unhappiness that made you risk surgery in the first place. And it *is* a risk. It's always a risk. Any kind of surgery is a risk. I'm married to a surgeon, so I ought to know. They've botched up a lot of faces. Permanently. And I knew all that beforehand.

Still, nothing could have stopped me from going ahead anyway. . . .

"When I look back at how I felt before, at how miserable I was every day of my life—well, I won't burden you with all that."

"You're supposed to," someone said. "That's why we're here, Isabel."

"Okay then. If that's how you feel. Maybe I'll learn something about myself—about why I went through all that crap. I don't think I've ever discussed my real reasons with anyone."

"Not even the plastic surgeon?"

"You mean Dr. Zimmer?"

"Whoever it was. . . ."

"God, no. He wouldn't give a damn what my reasons were. All those guys care about is their big fat fee. So I guess Dr. Zimmer simply assumed (as most men would) that I was motivated by sheer vanity, that my only concern was looking younger and prettier for my husband and for other men. He'd never understand that it was *fear* rather than vanity. Such a stupid morbid fear. And it's still there, but less than before. It first hit me when I turned forty and suddenly realized that I was now headed downhill, slipping closer and closer to death every hour of the day. I didn't really feel any older, certainly not in my body—but there was my face with all the evidence. Every new wrinkle and sag was another clue, another sign of death coming on—gradually but surely. Aging and dying have always gone together in my mind, and I've always had the most awful fear of death. Ever since I was a child. Somehow I've pictured the hereafter as the most horrible place you can possibly imagine. With gruesome horrible things, like hairy insects and snakes crawling in all that slime. Worse than hell. And my grandfather telling me—when I'd tell him my fears—that for me there is no hell."

55

"Is that what Jews think?" asked Jan.

"That's right," answered Selma. "At least that's what some of us are supposed to think."

"That must be sort of nice," said Jan. "Not having to worry where you'll go after you die."

"Anyway," said Isabel, continuing in the same flat voice that gained emphasis only when she paused. "I've always had that awful fear of death. So after my fortieth birthday I didn't want to look at my face anymore; I didn't want to see myself dying. Consequently, I would lie in bed all morning so I wouldn't have to look in the mirror to brush my teeth and fix my hair. And sometimes I would lie in bed till midafternoon, reading magazines and feeling sorry for myself. I thought about seeing a psychiatrist, started to call one at least four or five times, but always decided against it. I was too damned ashamed to tell anyone about my silly neurosis. . . . Finally I decided to get a new face—one that I could look at without thinking about dying. Now I know this will sound silly as hell, but, darn it, I'll have to admit that it sort of helped me. It really makes me feel younger."

"It should, Isabel," said Jan. "It's a beautiful job. I wouldn't have known you've had plastic surgery if you hadn't told us."

"Neither would I," someone added.

"So who cares what reasons you had?" said Selma with a careless lilt in her husky voice. "Personally, I never worry about dying, but I'd frankly like to change my face for vanity's sake—no matter what people think."

"Then getting old doesn't bother you?"

"Only because it makes me uglier, Trudy. Not only in my husband's eyes but also in my eyes. And let me tell you, he's not getting any prettier either. Instead of gray, he's getting bald, and the droop in his face I won't even mention. . . . "

"Hi, everybody." It was Ruth entering the room. "I

came after all. Decided it was chicken to stay away. Excuse the interruption, Selma. Please continue."

"So you can see that vanity strongly affects my feelings about getting old," said Selma. "Every new wrinkle is like another insult to nature. But there's something else that weighs heavily on my mind: It's menopause. I'm old enough now to start worrying about it, and my worries keep gnawing and gnawing away at me like some rats in an attic. Two of my aunts went through hell during menopause, one of them almost going insane. In fact, she's never completely recovered from that terrible period. She'd be sitting at the dinner table with my Uncle Stan, quietly eating, and suddenly she'd start trembling and shaking all over; then this weird catlike noise would force itself through her clenched teeth, and her eyes would bulge as if they might pop out of their sockets. And poor Uncle Stan, not knowing what else to do, would hug her with all his strength, repeating her name over and over again—Ellie, Ellie, Ellie—as if to remind himself, convince himself, that she was still the same person he had known before and not some strange demented female who had taken her place.

"Sometimes she would wake up in the middle of the night and rush around the house, upstairs and downstairs, opening all the windows and doors, complaining that she couldn't get enough air, that she was suffocating. Or she would get into her car and drive for hours and hours, aimlessly drifting from here to there until she'd run out of gas. Then, having forgotten her purse, she would somehow borrow a dime and call Uncle Stan, who would pick up a two-gallon can of gas and go to her rescue. What an awful time he had. There was always something strange and emotionally painful going on at their house, some minor crisis that would eventually involve my mother and dad."

57

"Did she ever get any kind of psychiatric treatment, Selma?"

"Some I guess. But nothing on a sustained basis. The two or three doctors she saw (one of them a shrink) simply told her that she was going through a tougher-than-usual menopause and that she'd eventually come out of it. So they'd give her a few pills, changing the colors now and then, and tell her to take it easy, relax, join a bridge club, take up gardening, knit something for somebody, just keep busy and stop thinking about yourself. As if it were that goddamned simple! Here you've got a bright, sensitive woman with a suddenly whacky metabolism that's causing all kinds of crazy short circuits and crossed circuits between her body and her brain, everything inside her going screwy and building up a million new pressures she's never felt before—and then some silly-ass doctor smugly tells her to relax and stop thinking about herself."

"Because those doctors don't give a damn!" snapped Trudy. "That's a female thing, so they couldn't care less. Now if menopause were a *male* sickness, they'd damned well care. There'd be billions for medical research to find some sort of treatment. But not as long as it's strictly female. Not a chance!"

"You couldn't be righter," said Rachel, her clear, firm voice somehow penetrating the babble of approval that instantly followed Trudy's moment of outrage. "They've got an institute for cancer research, institutes for kidney research, blood disease research, mental illness research, liver research, blindness research, and a lot more I won't bother to mention. But I've never heard of an institute for menopausal and menstrual research."

"And you're not likely to," Trudy added. "Not as long as men control all the money for medical research."

"But why don't they create an institute for impo-tency research?"

58

"Because they wouldn't want to admit—at least, not publicly—that the problem exists," said Graciela as the others laughed and shouted, "Right on!"

"Okay, sisters, time to get serious again," cautioned Selma. "We were talking about aging, menopause, and. . . ."

"Could I say something first?" asked Jan. "Before we go on with our main discussion?"

"Of course you can. That's why we're here, Jan."

"Well, I didn't want to get us off the track again, but there's something bothering me. I mean—well, about the discussions we've been having. They've really gotten to me. More than I expected. I'm acting so different now, especially at home. And it's really affecting my marriage. . . ."

"It's supposed to."

"Yes, but I'm not sure I can handle it. I thought it would be gradual. Then suddenly all this resentment against Ron starts boiling over. Sure, I've always bitched at him a little, but it was surface bitching, the kind any husband expects. You see it on television all the time. Nothing really serious. But lately I've been getting at him in different ways, and I've been listening to his wisecracks differently—as if . . . well—as if I've got a new pair of ears. I keep hearing new meanings in everything he says concerning marriage and women and even kids. And of course, it's had a strong effect on him. He's been looking at me with this funny look in his eyes, probably thinking that I've gone off my rocker. Like the other day, when my older boy was going off on a date, Ron asks him with that knowing man-to-man look, he asks, 'Are you getting any of that stuff?' And I really hit the roof. The minute Billie left I let Ron have it smack in the face, I called him a no-good sexist bastard and stomped outa the kitchen boiling mad. So he followed me upstairs, yelling my name and faking a stupid laugh. Then he came into the

59

bathroom and started telling me that it was only a harmless crack, the kind any dad makes to his older sons. And when I asked how he'd feel if some other dad asked the same question of some boy dating *our* daughter, he got angry as hell and accused me of having a dirty mind. Then he started asking me, 'What the shit are you dames talking about on Thursday nights?' and 'Why do you get sore at things you never got sore at before?' and finally 'Why can't you be the way you were?' But he wouldn't let me answer him. Just kept shouting over my head."

"Had you heard him make that crack before?"

"Which one?"

"When he asked your son, 'Are you getting any of that stuff?' Had he ever asked that before?"

"Oh, several times. It was their little joke. And I've got to admit that it used to seem cute to me. Dad and son having that man-to-man understanding—and Ron giving him his first box of rubbers. That sort of thing."

"I wonder how he'd feel if you had the reverse situation," said Rachel.

"What do you mean by reverse?"

"Well . . . supposing he saw you giving your teen-age daughter her first diaphragm—or the pill?"

"He'd die!" exclaimed Jan. "But he'd kill me first. He really would."

"That old double standard again," said Trudy.

"Anyway," Jan continued, "I've got some real problems at home, which I'm not sure I can handle. So maybe I'd better drop out for a while. Until I can get myself together."

"Oh, don't do that, Jan. You've got to stay," urged Graciela with considerable emphasis. "What you've just told us—I mean about your new reaction to such wisecracks—just shows how much you've gotten from these sessions, how much your consciousness has already been raised."

60

"That's true," added Selma. "That's a perfect example of what should be happening to all of us."

"I'm not so sure," said a voice we had not heard before. "You may be kidding yourself. You might be asking for a lot more than you can possibly handle. . . . Of course, I'm new here, and perhaps I shouldn't comment without knowing what you've dealt with in your first few meetings. But, from all I've heard tonight, I think you're falling into the same trap that most Women Libbers fall into—blaming all your problems on men. . . ."

The new voice belonged to Carol Mishkin, an editor with a major publishing company, whose husband produced television commercials for political candidates. John subsequently learned that Carol had been invited to the meeting as a "provisional member" of the group. Selma and Trudy had apparently been reluctant to admit any new members, fearing it would disrupt what Selma called "the nice harmony and unusual confidence we've developed among ourselves." But they had finally gone along with Rachel's request when it was generally agreed that Carol would have a "provisional" status. Judging from the immediate reaction to her initial comments, Carol was obviously in rough waters from the very outset.

"You certainly are presumptuous," said Selma in the cool, well-modulated voice of someone deliberately restraining her emotions. "If you *had* been here and if you had listened attentively without making snap judgments, you certainly couldn't assume that we're blaming men for everything."

"That's right," said Graciela, her manner equally cool and direct. "We've been pretty damned candid about our own failings. Painfully so. But we certainly can't express our feelings as women without mentioning

—and analyzing—how men have affected us. After all, this *is* a male-dominated society."

"Well, maybe I'm wrong for spouting off so soon," said Carol defensively. "I simply assumed that we're supposed to be honest with ourselves."

"We are," snapped Rachel. "But I told you before this meeting started—as we were driving over—that we're not supposed to criticize and analyze what someone else is saying. That we've got to be supportive of each other. Not critical."

"Then what's the point of all this?" asked Carol, her voice on the verge of laughter. "If I can't analyze what you're saying, how can I be of any help to you?"

"You're not here to help *me*, sweetie. You're here to help yourself. And as long as you keep saying 'you' instead of 'I,' this isn't going to work for you. In other words, I've got to find out how *I* feel about myself as a woman, how *I* feel (I mean really feel) about my husband, my kids, my home, my job, my friends. And when I listen to Trudy say her thing, I've got to dig into myself to find out how *I* felt (or feel) about the same circumstances when they happen to me."

"So what's wrong with a little honest criticism?" Carol persisted.

"Because it's usually egotistical—and also presumptuous, I might add."

"But what could be more egotistical than all this I-I-I business you're talking about? Seems awfully self-centered to me."

"Not if it's genuine self-concern, instead of the conceit you're thinking about."

"What's the difference?"

"Oh, come on, Carol. You're not that dense. There's a big difference between someone who's concerned, deeply concerned, about her own fears, her hopes, her self-deceptions, her real motives about this and that—as compared to someone who is merely self-centered and egotistical, who wouldn't dare probe beneath her own surface. That's the difference."

"I'm still not convinced," said Carol. "But I'll keep my mouth shut if that's how you all feel."

"Talk all you want," said Trudy. "Just don't get analytical about someone else. Personally, I'd like to hear what you think about yourself."

"Perhaps you will," was the chilly response.

"Okay, sisters, let's get back to my damned menopause," said Selma, resuming her usual jocular manner. "Or someone else's menopause. I guess I've expressed all my worries about it. How about you, Rachel?"

"I'm like you, Selma, I've got the same worries about menopause. So when you were telling us about your aunt's problems, that really got to me. In a very personal way. It reminded me of the awful time my mother had. . . . Poor mom. I can still remember the strange terrified look in her face, especially her eyes. That feverish neon glint in her pupils, the constant tremor around the edges of her tightly closed mouth, her fists so tightly clenched I thought her knuckles would crack. Then suddenly she'd lapse into a state of nothingness—her eyes totally blank and unresponsive, her mouth slack and half open, with a web of saliva near each end.

"But it wasn't always one extreme or another, thank God. She'd also have these in-between periods of comparative normality, sometimes for two or three weeks at a stretch. We'd think it's all over now, she's finally gotten through it. And my dad (oh, how that poor man suffered) would take us all out to dinner—to celebrate at some fancy restaurant, insisting we all drink a glass of champagne and holding mom's hand most of the night. Then one evening, just as we were getting ready for another one of daddy's celebration dinners, I saw my mother's

63

hand shaking as she started to put on her lipstick, suddenly missing her upper lip and smearing what looked like a red mustache—or half of one—right under her nose. Then letting out a weird scream that started like a soft growl, and slashing the mirror with red streaks until she couldn't see her face anymore. . . .

"We could never predict what might happen to mom during those long two years that actually seemed like a whole decade. She went to four or five different doctors, and it was always the same story: 'You're having a difficult menopause, but you'll probably snap out of it pretty soon. Just relax and try not to think about it?' Plus another supply of uppers and downers, pills and liquid medicine which tasted like fish oil, she said. Yet nothing, nothing at all, seemed to help. She'd be hysterical a few days, almost normal for a week or so, then hysterical again, followed by a brief or prolonged depression, then normal or hysterical. On and on and on, with no predictable sequence to give dad or me some warning, some clue to what might happen tomorrow or the next day.

"This happened when I was fourteen and fifteen years old, which would have been miserable for me even if mom had been perfectly normal. My menstrual periods were awful. These terrible cramps and nervous tension for five or six days, sometimes coming on at exactly the same time mom was having one of her sieges of hysteria. Poor dad must have—God, I don't know what he must have gone through, with both of us screaming at each other or sulking around the house like sick animals. He was incredibly patient with both of us. Especially in the morning, which was always the worst part of the day for me.

"Before her menopause, mom would always get up to make me a hot breakfast, either french toast or these marvelous scrambled eggs with mushrooms. But after her cycle began, my dad immediately took over the breakfast chores, realizing that mom and I would inevitably get into a big argument, both of us being so tense and irritable that almost any insignificant trifle could lead to an explosion. But he was different. Instead of reacting to my usual early-morning bitchiness, he'd simply ignore my complaints and never snap back at me. He'd pad into the kitchen whistling or singing half-finished verses from old, old songs he couldn't fully remember, meanwhile overcooking the eggs, burning the toast, and periodically reminding me to hurry so I wouldn't miss the school bus. With all that good cheer, how could I complain about the food he cooked?

"Remembering all that," said Rachel, her voice softer and more pensive than before, "I sure hope my daughter's away at college or married by the time my menopause rolls around. I'm afraid I'll be a real bitch to live with."

"Maybe not," said Ruth, expressing a rather timid hope. "There might be some miracle pill or special treatment by then."

"Don't count on it," Trudy cut in.

"There's always a possibility," Ruth insisted. "I'll bet someone is doing research on the problem. . . . But that's not my biggest worry—I mean menopause. The thing that worries me most is old age itself. I keep remembering all those ancient people—mostly women— at Miami Beach on my first and only vacation in Florida. All those flabby pale bodies in those awful I'm-staying-young bathing suits. Some of you have mentioned how much you hate wrinkly old faces, but I think ugly bodies are a lot worse. Saggy breasts that hang like empty sacks, with nipples that remind you of bleached prunes. And varicose veins scribbled on dead-white flesh; flabs of fat that wobble with every step or skeleton limbs with no fat at all, just creaky bones and loose skin. Those crooked shapeless bodies shuffling around in slow motion—the timid, groping movements of a blind man turning a strange corner. It wore me out just looking at them. They also depressed me, depressed me more than anything I'd ever seen—because I could clearly imagine myself looking and acting exactly the same way in less than twenty years.

"I got so damned gloomy my husband cut short our Florida vacation and took me to Mexico City for the last ten days. He wanted to try Acapulco but changed his mind when I reminded him that we might see a lot of naked old ladies on that beach. And ever since then (for about three or four years) I've studiously avoided going any place where I might see old people in swimming suits."

"You seem to get more depressed by old women than by old—"

"Oh, definitely!" exclaimed Ruth. "Women are much uglier than men when they get past fifty. And a lot more so after sixty. It's our darned breasts that get so awful. That loose useless flesh hanging down to our stomachs. As a matter of fact, most of our female flesh gets flabby and shapeless."

"Now you're getting *me* depressed," complained Rachel in a half-kidding tone. "I'm liable to drive into the ocean when this meeting is over."

"Strange that you should say that," said Ruth, apparently missing the intended humor. "I once told my husband that I'm not going to let myself get old, that I'll drive off a cliff when I'm fifty-five. But of course I was only kidding. I'm too much of a coward to do anything like that."

"How about you, Graciela?" asked Selma. "You looked amused when Ruth mentioned suicide."

"It wasn't the suicide bit that amused me," Graciela hastily responded. "It was something else. I was actually thinking about myself and wondering how I'd look without the big droopy breasts *I've* got. A lot better, I guess. In fact, we'd all look better *without* boobs. But I wouldn't wait till we're fifty to get rid of them, Ruth. They start drooping a lot sooner than that. . . ."

"But we'd look so freakish!" protested Jan, apparently thinking Graciela was dead serious. "I don't think I'd recognize myself."

"So what's wrong with that?" asked Selma with an audible chuckle. "I'm not so stuck on myself. Especially with my boobs. Now, if I had nice little tits like Trudy, I wouldn't—"

"Stop it, for Christ's sake!" yelled Jan. "It's nothing to joke about. My mother had cancer, and they had to remove her right breast. It looked awful. So it's nothing to joke about. Believe me."

"I do," said Selma, her voice suddenly flat and serious. "I only joke to hide my own fears. Both my mother and my aunt had a breast removed less than a year apart. . . . My mother had a particularly hard time. But even she managed to joke about it. The minute my dad came into the recovery room she grinned at him and said, 'You should ask my father to return half the dowry.' Then dad reminded her that it was *he* who had gotten the dowry from my grandfather. 'So he had to pay you to take me,' mom said, still grinning. 'You should have demanded twice as much, Max. You got only half a woman.'

"That's when the joke turned sour. That kind of humor always does. But we're a compulsive family, Jan. We never know when to stop."

"I'm sorry," said Jan, fumbling for words. "It was only—I mean I wasn't criticizing your sense of humor, Selma. I really envy the way you can laugh at almost anything."

"Kind of you to say that, Jan. But I'll have to admit

I went overboard on the breast business. I'll try to control myself."

"I don't think you should," said Trudy. "That's your nature, Selma. Why suppress it? Anyway, it's your wisecracks that keep the rest of us from going overboard on the serious side."

"She's right," added Rachel. "If you don't keep me laughing, sweetie, I'll cry my eyes out. 'Cause that's my nature—crying. Now let's get on with the show."

"Okay, it's Trudy's turn."

"We'll have a coffee break first," said Selma.

There was a ten-minute interval of chitchat about a recent storm and flooded basements, then Trudy's crisp Smith-Vassar-or-Wellesley voice came into sharper focus as the other voices faded.

". . . so that menopause and physical ugliness aren't my principal concerns when I think about old age. I'm mostly worried about dependency. I mean economic and psychological dependency. For the past two hours I've been thinking about the summer I spent in Mexico City, living in a *pension* near the Hotel Genova, which everyone called Menopause Mansion because most of its permanent residents were these old American widows who sat around the lobby like mourners at a perpetual wake. Their husbands had died and left them just enough money to live in shabby gentility in places like Mexico. Back home they'd live in genteel poverty suddenly shunned by old acquaintances whose husbands hadn't died yet. Old widows are such a drag to have around. Even their children and grandchildren studiously avoid them."

"That's so true," said Ruth. "I'm always avoiding my mother—won't even answer her phone calls. I feel so guilty about her. But Walter can't stand her anymore, and—quite frankly—neither can I."

"They're so damned *kvetchy*, always complaining,"

said Selma. "Especially my husband's mother. I'd like to send her to Florida. Someplace like St. Petersburg or that hotel in Mexico, but she'd be afraid to eat there."

"No need to worry about eating at the Hotel Genova," Trudy assured her. "It's the safest food in Mexico—boiled, bland, and tasteless. Just like hospital food. No Mexican ever eats there, and those poor old biddies never eat anywhere else. In fact, they seldom wander outside their rooms or the lobby. All day long and most of the evening they sit in these hand-carved colonial chairs, quietly chatting with each other about the same things, over and over and over again, like cows rechewing their cud. But as they're talking, their pale anxious eyes keep shifting around, hoping to spot some tourist from back home. Poor things, they're so nostalgic and yet so hungry for new acquaintances that they'll grab any opening for a conversation with almost any stranger: 'Did I hear you say Denver? . . . Did you get that blouse in Oaxaca? . . . You look just like my daughter. . . . My, isn't it warm today?' And I, being a sentimental idiot, would let myself get dragged into the dreariest conversations about the servant problem in Dallas, the high price of liver in Chicago, the mugging problem in Los Angeles, or the added tax on Geritol in Mexico."

"What were *you* doing in the hotel?"

"I'd be passing through the lobby to get *Time* or *Newsweek* at the newsstand, and one of them would glom onto me. They had me tagged as one of those good-listener types. But I'd come away feeling awfully depressed and vulnerable. Their damned loneliness was sort of contagious."

"I know how you feel," said Jan. "My aunt's like that. She comes by to see me twice a week (always in the afternoon because Ron so obviously resents her), and whenever she's around, the whole house seems to get

69

gloomy. It's like she's carrying it around with her—all that gloom."

"How about old men?" someone asked.

"There aren't as many around," answered Trudy. "They're mostly women. Everyone knows we live longer than men."

"Which ain't no special advantage," said Rachel, switching to a ghetto dialect she occasionally used to stress certain views. "Particularly when yo' poor 'n' black. I've seen some poor old sisters in Harlem that almost break your heart. Working all their lives in other people's homes, taking all kinds of shit from the Man, then having to ask for welfare when they're too old to lift a hand without feeling the misery in their bones, and having to listen to all that crap about lazy shiftless niggers. So you'll have to excuse me for not shedding too many tears for those po' white ladies in that Mexican hotel. . . ."

"I guess you're right," mumbled Trudy after a ten- or fifteen-second silence. "There are people who suffer much more than others; but you'll have to admit that most widows—black or white—have a pretty lousy situation."

"They're everywhere," said Isabel. "You see thousands of poor Jewish widows living in Miami Beach, most of them south of the big shopping area. Living in smelly little rooms in those shabby hotels, where even the elevators smell of old cabbage. Or you see them eating alone in a kosher cafeteria, hunched over a bowl of matzoh-ball soup solemnly munching the dough with their false teeth as they slowly turn to stare out the window, hoping they'll see a familiar face. Then back to their crappy rooms to reread for the hundredth time a month-old postcard with seventeen words of love from a daughter or son in Forest Hills or Denver or even Beverly Hills."

Her soft-voiced, yet bitter description provoked an acute reaction from Graciela. "I could never live like that. I'd rather kill myself. What's more, I can't understand their sons and daughters abandoning them that way. That sure doesn't happen with Mexicans or Chicanos. . . ."

"It doesn't?"

"Never," answered Graciela. "You won't find any groups of Mexican widows exiled in the hotel lobbies or old ladies' homes."

"Then where do you keep them?"

"They live with one of their children—generally with the oldest son or daughter's family. Or in an apartment close to at least one of her kids."

"That's a pretty nice deal for the widow," said Isabel. "But how does her daughter-in-law feel about it? Any resentment?"

"Some, I guess. But she expects it. And she also knows that she won't be abandoned when *she* becomes a widow. So it evens out in the long run."

Selma was less than fully persuaded. "Wellll," she demurred, drawling the *l*, "I'm not sure I could accept such an arrangement. Alvin's mother is quite a bitch— even when she's on good behavior. And I wouldn't want to live with any of my future daughters-in-law, whoever they may be. Particularly if their daughters are as bratty as mine. We'd have three generations of bitches under one roof. Hah! I'd rather be a lonely widow, thank you."

"Maybe you're right," said Trudy. "I sure don't want to be a burden on my kids, but I'd hate to live alone in a shabby hotel, surrounded by a bunch of lonely, self-pitying widows and feeling myself getting more and more senile every day. . . ."

"Now that's what I'm worried about—senility." It was Rachel breaking in. "I watched my grandmother growing senile—her memory fading, her eyes becoming blurred and watery, her hands getting shakier and shakier, everything coming apart. She might tell me something one minute and a half hour later repeat the same damned thing, often repeating herself ten times in a single day."

"That's exactly what happened to my mother, poor thing," said Ruth. "She'd tell me the same story over and over til I'd want to scream."

"They may call it second childhood," Rachel added. "But that's a *kind* way to put it. No child is that pitiful—and certainly not as boring."

Suddenly there was a muffled sob and several worried exclamations, then Isabel's faltering anguished voice: "My God—oh, my God, is that all we have to look forward to? Is old age nothing but loneliness and gloom?"

"Of course not," soothed Rachel. "I've known a lot of fairly happy old people. Some of them widows with very little money. It's mostly a matter of attitude . . . and luck, I guess. I'm sure not going to quit when I'm sixty. No matter how ugly I am."

"I'm with you, Rachel," said Selma. "But I'm getting myself a little insurance."

"Insurance?"

"That's what I said—but not the kind of insurance you're thinking about. It's more personal. I'm going back to work next year, back to my practice as a psychologist. I'll get another woman to take care of my kids."

"Good for you," someone said approvingly.

"There's something else I'm going to do," she added. "I might as well confess (since we're being so honest with each other) that if my husband should double-cross me and die before I do, then I'm going to invest in some plastic surgery."

"A face-lift?"

"Why not?" asked Selma. "And maybe I'll get a booby-lift—if it doesn't cost too much."

72

They all laughed when she mentioned the breast lifting and someone yelled, "So will I!" But Selma's suddenly solemn voice quickly silenced them.

"That sounds like a big joke, all right. But I didn't mean to be funny—not about that. I guess that it slipped out just then. What I said about plastic surgery . . . I've been thinking about it a long time. Because, quite frankly, I've been worried about getting bags under my eyes and a flabby face and my husband taking off with a young *shiksa*. It's not that I love him so much—it's just that I'm really afraid to be left alone. So I don't want a divorce, and I don't want him to die before I do. And please forgive me for ending this session on such a low note."

"That's okay, sweetie," said Rachel in her most comforting voice. "No one expects you to be funny all the time."

Since Carol Mishkin had made no comments during the last two hours of this meeting, I asked John if he knew what had happened to her. "She apparently left just after the second coffee break," he told me. "My wife subsequently mentioned some newcomer who had rubbed everyone the wrong way on her very first appearance and that they had given her the big freeze, causing her to leave before the meeting was over. So we've got to assume it was Carol."

This impression was subsequently verified when John and his wife met a Mr. and Mrs. Mishkin at a charity dinner, all of them having been assigned to the same table.

"I believe I've met your wife," Mrs. Mishkin said to John as the various couples introduced themselves. "About three months ago."

Then turning to John's wife with a cool smile, she asked, "How is the female Mafia doing these days?"

73

"Same as ever," was the equally cool reply. "We're killing our usual quota."

"I can well imagine," Mrs. Mishkin purred. "Probably with arsenic and old lace."

"Just arsenic. The old lace is sort of passé."

With that rejoinder their conversation came to an abrupt end, according to John, and the two women deliberately avoided each other for the rest of the evening.

IV

Sex in the Suburbs

The only unnatural sex act is that which you cannot perform.

—ALFRED KINSEY

"I GUESS this will be our most difficult session," said Selma at the beginning of the third meeting. "Most people are pretty squeamish about sex. But we've got to be honest with ourselves. So I might as well start by confessing that my sex life is rather blah. Probably because my husband's such a lousy fuck."

"Must you use that word?" protested Ruth.

"Okay, Ruthie—let's just call him a lousy screw. You're prissy as hell for a big girl."

"I guess I am, Selma. I'm sorry to break in that way. It's just that—"

"You'll get used to it," someone said. "Fuck is just another word. You hear it everywhere. Even in the movies."

"Yes, I know that. But I'm still having trouble getting used to it. I mean among women."

"Why don't you say it a few times?" suggested Graciela. "It's easy. Fuck, fuck, fuck—just like that."

"Well. . . ."

"Don't force her," said Jan, her soft, husky voice filling the sudden void. "I know exactly how she feels. I never use it myself—except when I'm boiling mad.

75

That's when Ron really blows up. He says only whores talk that way."

"That's what most men say," said Graciela. "If you can't say it, you can't think it. That's how naïve most men are. They try to control our minds by controlling our tongues."

"They're naïve in all kinds of ways," added Selma. "Especially about sex. Either naïve or uptight. But I guess my husband is more uptight than naïve. That's why he's so lousy in bed. He knows what a clitoris is for, but he can't bring himself to fondle one—at least not mine."

"Isn't he an analyst?"

"That's right, Trudy. Alvin the anal-yst, if I may repeat my own pun."

"But aren't psychoanalysts supposed to know about such—"

"Well, that's the word all right—the exact word. They're *supposed* to know. But Alvin, like most analysts, got his initial training when most people believed all that Freudian crap about clitoral and vaginal orgasms. And I myself (as a practicing psychologist before my own kids' problems forced me to give it up), I also accepted that nonsense. As a matter of fact, I was looking through some of my old textbooks last night, and I want to read you some passages I marked. Listen to this, for example. From Freud's *Three Essays on the Theory of Sexuality*:

> With few exceptions, I, myself, doubt whether the female child can be seduced to anything but clitoris masturbation. The frequent spontaneous discharges of sexual excitement in little girls manifest themselves in a twitching of the clitoris, and its frequent. . . .

"Well, I'll skip that and go—"

"But I want to hear that, Selma! At least the end of the sentence."

76

"Okay. Just the end of that paragraph. . . ."

. . . and its frequent erections (the clitoris), enable the girl to understand correctly even without any instructions the sexual manifestations of the other sex. . . .

"Then he talks about females having to mature by transferring from clitoral to vaginal stimulation. Listen to this":

It often takes some time before this transference is accomplished, and during this transition the young wife remains anesthetic. This anesthesia may become permanent if the clitoric zone refuses to give up its excitability; a condition brought on by profuse sexual activities in infantile life. It is known that anesthesia in women is often only apparent and local. They are anesthetic at the vaginal entrance, but not at all unexcitable through the clitoris or even through other zones. Besides these erogenous causes of anesthesia, there are also psychic causes, likewise determined by the repression.

If the transference of the erogenous excitability from the clitoris to the vaginal entrance succeeds, the woman then changes her leading zone for the future sexual activity; the man, on the other hand, retains his from childhood. The main determinants for the woman's preference for neuroses, especially for hysteria, lie in this change of the leading zone as well as in the repression of puberty. These determinants are, therefore, most intimately connected with the nature of femininity.

While the primacy of the genital zone is being established through the processes of puberty, the erected penis in the man imperiously points towards the new sexual aim, *i.e.*, towards the penetration of a cavity which excites the genital zone. . . .

"Imperiously points!" Rachel sneered. "I'll bet the males liked that one."

"Is that why he accused women of suffering from penis envy?" asked Trudy.

"Exactly," Selma answered. "Freud looked upon us as mutilated males yearning for a lost pecker. And any desire for clitoral stimulation was taken as proof of that theory."

"He went further than that," said Graciela. "At least his followers did. They simply concluded that clitoral women were mean neurotic bitches with masculine tendencies. Whereas women who had vaginal orgasms were feminine, mature, sort of maternal, and *normal,* of course."

"So that makes me an abnormal bitch," said Selma.

"But why?" someone started to ask.

"Well, that's their notion—not mine," Selma continued. "And Alvin's right with them, a typical old-fashioned Freudian. That's why he can't satisfy me. He knows I'm clitoral, but he won't touch me there. It's a real hangup he's got. So once in a while—as we're about to have sex, which ain't often—I masturbate a little. But he hates that. Really hates it. No outward objection, mind you, but I can feel his body stiffening. Sometimes his prick will start to droop. It'll droop just as my clitoris starts to erect. . . ."

"You're certainly clinical, Selma," said Rachel.

"How else can I explain it? After all, we're supposed to be frank and specific in these sessions. Otherwise, we'll be talking in circles—in meaningless abstractions."

"Right on, sweetie. Excuse the interruption."

"Okay. Now, as I was saying about my husband, his clitoral phobia relates only to me. He may be okay with other women. And I'm sure he advises all his men patients to pay more attention to their wives' clitori or

78

clitorises or whatever in hell the plural is. But that doesn't help me very much."

"Have you discussed it with him?"

"I've tried to, Jan, but he always puts me off. He gets this silly-ass superior grin on his face and quickly changes the subject."

"Don't men ever talk about sex?" asked Trudy.

"Not with their wives," said Selma. "Certainly not in a personal way. Not even analysts. That's why they have such crappy marriages. They're always splitting up."

"Really?"

"They sure do, Trudy. I'll bet psychoanalysts have the highest divorce rate of any profession."

"That's hard to believe. I mean—"

"Not when you really think about it," said Selma. "After all, most analysts and psychologists are drawn to the profession because of their own fucked-up minds. I've never met so many weirdo students as there were in my graduate psych courses. And I was one of them—but not as weird as some of them."

"Is that where you met your husband?"

"Precisely. But he was already an instructor—you know, the young genius type. Yet he had this phobia, this screwy fantasy, he kept telling me about. Even then. He was always having this same dream—mostly in day-dreams—about a fantastic affair with this beautiful blond *shiksa.* He kept telling me about her, about how regular her features were, how small her nose was without plastic surgery. He could tell I'd had a nose bob (anybody could), but that bastard kept telling me about this *shiksa's* nice Nordic features. So—quite logically—I had to marry the *shnook.* Save him from his fantasies with a few good screws. I'd fuck him into reality."

"Did you?" asked Rachel.

79

"Hell, no. He's still having the same dream, the same fantasy. Every time we see a young blonde, one of those perfect *shiksa* types with long hair and narrow hips and skinny little nose, Alvin turns and stares at her—his eyes glazing over."

"He ought to buy one," suggested Rachel.

"I've told him that, sweetie. We were in Vegas a couple of years ago, and I pointed out this beautiful hooker in the next booth. But he wouldn't go for her. 'The money angle would ruin it,' he told me. It had to be real. One of those true romances like in a pulp magazine, with Alvin chasing her through the woods or down the beach. He's a regular Portnoy, my Alvin—with a pot-belly and bad breath. And even if he did get his dream *shiksa*, I don't think he'd screw her. That would spoil the whole thing. . . ."

"How do you know that?"

"Because he's never mentioned sex with her, Rachel. It's always hand holding or reading poetry on the grass, or some other virginal crap. . . . I'll never figure out why I've stayed with him. Except that he's an awfully funny guy—even when he's talking about his *shiksa*. He actually kids himself."

"Maybe it's all a put-on."

"How so?"

"Maybe he's only pretending to have that fantasy. Just to goad you."

"Well, he's certainly that kind of bastard. But he's not that good a faker, Rachel. I'm afraid it's for real. Though I wish it weren't."

"At least it's a girl he's fantasizing about," said Trudy with a certain urgency in her high-pitched voice. "My husband seems to have this hangup on young *boys*, but he never talks about it. He's been that way for several years. Every time he sees a handsome teen-ager he gets this funny look in his eyes, and his mouth starts twitching. And sometimes he'll find some reason to talk with them—just any stupid reason. It's like that movie I saw the other night, the one that's supposed to be about Gustav Mahler."

"You mean *Death in Venice.*"

"Yes, that's the one. But I'm afraid John has gone much further than Mahler did. I'm sure he's gone beyond the looking stage, at least two or three times."

"How would you know, Trudy?"

"Well . . . there's been nothing I could point to, nothing obvious. Mostly these feelings I've gotten on certain occasions when John has suddenly disappeared for a few hours—sometimes two or three days. Then coming home with guilt written all over his face. And something in his voice, a kind of stutter."

"Couldn't it be another woman?"

"God, I wish it were, Jan. But I doubt it. Because they always happen—these sudden disappearances—just after he's been staring at one of these teen-age boys. And there's one other . . . well, another clue, you might call it: When he comes back he's talking in a different way. The way homosexuals talk. Sort of prissy and too precise. He also does that when he's had a few drinks. As if he's imitating Clifton Webb—that limp-wrist sort of thing. It's so damned different from his usual dull, plodding manner."

"Have you ever asked him where he's been?" asked Graciela. "I mean, when he's been away for a couple of days."

"Oh, I always do," said Trudy. "And it's always the same answer: He's got to get away because of our son. Ronnie's illness depresses him, he says. And Ronnie's his excuse for never having sex with me anymore. He's sure it's genetic. But, of course, I am, too. I'll never want another baby. I wouldn't risk it. Never. Not when I see Ronnie. So we're even on the sex business. Neither of us

81

wants to risk it. Maybe his only out is a homosexual thing. And—who knows?—I may end up the same way. It's happened with other women, I guess."

"It sure has," said Rachel. "You're looking at one, Trudy. I've had two lesbian affairs in the last five years. And one before I married Jerry—when I was still in college. But I don't want any of you sisters to get worried. None of you are my type—"

Laughter and giggling in the background.

"I like them young and virginal. My first one was blond and willowy—like that *shiksa* your husband's been dreaming about, Selma. I guess we've got the same tastes. Funny thing, though, it was Sharon who came after me. We were in this play together. Both of us were young witches in Arthur Miller's *The Crucible*, about a year after it closed on Broadway, the best damned production we ever did at the university. . . . Well, anyway, Sharon used to stare at me the way lovers ought to stare. Still, it made me sort of uncomfortable. Then she made some remark about my skin. She really dug black, I guess."

"You're closer to caramel than black, Rachel," someone observed.

"Well, I'm certainly an identifiable Negro," said Rachel. "And I'd just as soon call myself black."

"I'll bet that wasn't always so," said Graciela with a hint of mockery.

"No, I guess not, Gracie. But as a newly militant Chicana, you know what I'm getting at."

"Okay, okay," protested Selma. "Let's save the ethnic stuff for another meeting. I want to hear more about your little Sharon."

"I figured you would," said Rachel. "So let's get back to her. Now, as I was saying, she made the first approach. She started walking back to my dorm with me after rehearsals, going way out of her way. She lived in

one of the sorority houses on the opposite end of the
campus. Walking right next to me in the dark, way after
sunset, and occasionally brushing her arm against mine.
Sometimes her hand touching mine. Then one evening,
as she was reciting a few lines of poetry (probably Millay
or Emily Dickinson), she pressed her hand into mine and
held it a long while, turning to look at me with her blue
eyes shining in the moonlight. Tears in them. Then,
without saying a word, she put both arms around me and
tenderly embraced me. 'I love you,' she said, almost
losing her voice. 'I love you, Rachel, and I can't help
myself.' Then she softly drew away and suddenly took off,
sobbing as she ran.

"So I phoned her that night and told her not to feel
guilty, not to run away anymore. That maybe I felt the
same way about her. Well, after a while we started to get
rid of our guilts and our shyness. And then our fear. We
saw each other every day. Ate together, studied together,
went to movies together, took long, long walks together,
holding hands and never giving a damn who saw us.
Finally, we slept together. And that was beautiful, tender
and beautiful. Her aunt had this lovely cabin in the
mountains, and that's where we spent our first weekend
together. Like young lovers, like a honeymoon couple. I
particularly remember the first time she made love to me.
How I nearly went mad when she started fondling my
clitoris—with her fingers at first and then her mouth. But
so gently it felt like butterfly wings. No man can ever be
that loving, that tender. . . ."

"My gosh," someone exclaimed. "I've got goose
bumps."

"And I'm blushing," said Jan. "I'm really blushing.
But please go on."

"Anyway, I still remember those nights whenever
Jerry makes love to me. He's such an awful brute. Like

Marlon Brando in *Streetcar*. All muscle and no soul. Yet he's a lot more tender than some actors I've known. Either they're rapists or faggots."

"Have you known many?"

"The only men I ever saw when I was acting Off Broadway and the summer circuits. I never got to Broadway."

"But your husband has."

"Yep, he's been in three or four Broadway plays and a bunch of television shows. That's where I met him—in one of those crappy soap operas. I was his maid, his cute little half-ass maid. But they paid me for that. Now I'm doing it for free."

"That's pretty funny," said Selma. "From a paid maid to a laid maid."

"That's a good one, sweetie," said Rachel. "But the actual getting laid ain't so funny. Jerry makes love as if it's an act of revenge. Maybe against his mother, for all I know. But it hurts like hell, mostly because there's very little foreplay. 'I can't wait,' he tells me. 'I can't wait for all that preliminary shit.' And maybe he's right. He probably can't wait. Because he generally comes after two or three strokes. Then off he comes—not giving a damn how I feel. Groaning like a wounded pig and rushing for the bathroom to get a towel. He never seems to think about the damned towel before coming to bed. Neither do I, because I never know when he's planning to do anything. It's always his decision. And, quite frankly, I'm just as happy when he leaves me alone."

"Is that what drove you into the two lesbian affairs you mentioned earlier?" asked Isabel.

"No, I can't honestly say that. I guess I'm what the menfolk call a natural switch-hitter. I dig both sexes. So I'd probably gone ahead with both those women even if I'd been married to someone less brutal than Jerry. As a

matter of fact, I've had affairs with two or three men who
were very gentle. My first husband (he was a black
dentist and the father of my teen-age boy), well, he was a
very gentle person. Very considerate."

"How about the two women?"

"Well, one of them is married to this other actor that
Jerry knows. The four of us saw each other quite a bit
two summers ago. We shared a beach house for two
months. Just the kind of setup for almost any hanky-
panky you can think of—lez, homo, or switcheroo. Elsa
and I chose the lez scene, and I don't know what the boys
did. They were certainly away a lot. Consequently—with
all our teen-agers off to camp—we had the house all to
ourselves. So one thing led to another. First, a little
guarded feeling-around conversation. Then some casual
not-so-accidental touching of hands and thighs. Then the
whole bit. With none of that guilt and hysteria that you
get between unmarried lesbians or young girls."

"Is that what happened between you and Sharon?"
asked Graciela.

"Yes, I'm afraid so. That whole thing turned sour.
Especially when her mother found out. She called me a
nigger bitch and threatened to tell the dean of women.
But she finally cooled off and sent Sharon off to Europe
for her senior year. And this other woman I had an affair
with, this thirty-year-old painter, also got hysterical after
a while. She wanted me to leave Jerry and my two
kids—started to demand it. She wasn't satisfied with just
a little sex. She wanted the whole number."

"You've certainly lived a lot," said Ruth. "I feel so
terribly naïve. Like one of those stupid little girls that
Louisa May Alcott used to write about. I've really been
living in a cocoon—all my life. Even now."

"How about your husband?"

"I guess Walter's about the same. Except that he's a

Horatio Alger character, the poor boy who made good by working twelve or sixteen hours a day. He still does. He's literally married to his law office."

"Where did you meet him, Ruth?"

"Well . . . you're going to laugh at this, but it's the truth. I met Walter at a church supper. And I guess we've never left that church supper. Neither one of us has changed much. We're both dull, I guess. Dull and reliable. I can't conceive of Walter having an affair. Certainly not with his secretary. She's duller than I am. Duller and older. She's the most typical old maid you've ever seen. Steel-rimmed glasses, thin pinched lips, sensible no-nonsense shoes, and always wearing a gray dress. They're a perfect match in a way. Because Walter has always worn a gray suit, lighter in the summer and thicker in winter but almost the same shade."

"Nothing mod?"

"Oh, never! He'd never wear any of these new fashions. Certainly not the loud ties and shirts. He's conservative all the way. Even in politics—especially politics. And that's where we differ. You see, I've been sort of a peacenik. At least that's what he's been calling me since I joined the peace movement. I couldn't stand the Vietnam War anymore. All that horrible slaughter. Particularly the bombing and the napalm. But Walter sticks up for Nixon. Anything Nixon does is perfect in Walter's eyes. So when I started showing him all those pictures of kids being murdered by bombs and chemicals, he simply turned his eyes. Propaganda, he calls it. But I kept going to those rallies, in spite of Walter. And that's where I met Trudy—at one of the rallies. And later on she took me to a Women's Lib meeting. Which finally led me into this group. But I haven't told him about this. . . ."

"What would he do?"

"I don't really care, Selma. But I guess he'd be

pretty shocked. Especially if he could hear what we've been talking about tonight. We could never talk about sex this way. Never, never, never. So I could never use that word you wanted me to say, Graciela."

"You mean fuck?"

"Yes, that's the one."

"Why don't you try it sometime?"

"He'd kill me. He really would."

"Well, you've certainly slept together, haven't you? At least as often as Nixon and Pat."

Much laughter and inaudible joking in the background, then Ruth's voice again.

"Probably more," said Ruth. "But not much more. Walter is always so tired when he finally comes home. Tired and grumpy. So I've always had to initiate things, I mean on the few occasions we've been together. And it's been awfully embarrassing for me—having to start it all and feeling sort of cheap and vulgar. That's how he's made me feel sometimes. Cheap and vulgar. So I end up going down to the den. To watch television—almost until dawn. Feeling lonely and sorry for myself. And wanting to masturbate the way I did before my mother caught me. But finally just sitting there, clutching the armrests of my big chair, staring at the Late Late Show until I'm too exhausted to stay awake. Then getting up to fix his damned breakfast. Oatmeal and dry toast. The same thing every morning—three hundred and sixty-five days a year—oatmeal and dry toast."

"I guess I'm fairly well off," said Jan, breaking the long silence that followed Ruth's final words. "My husband's a mean, chauvinistic Italian slob, but I'll have to admit he's great in bed. He makes me come all the time. Now, I'm not saying Ron is what you call tender or gentle, but he certainly does all that's necessary to make a woman climax—sometimes more than once."

"Are they clitoral or vaginal orgasms?" asked Selma.

"I don't know, frankly. And I really don't care as long as he makes me come."

"Okay, I realize that, Jan—but does your clitoris get more stimulated than—"

"Come on, Selma," yelled Rachel. "You're analyzing. You're the one who's been harping on that."

"But I'm *not* analyzing, I'm merely asking questions. For clarif—"

"That's still analyzing," said Graciela. "You're cross-examining like a female Perry Mason."

"Okay, I'm sorry," said Selma, a chuckle in her voice. "I'm just so damned curious. And a little envious, I guess."

"Go on, Jan," someone urged.

"Well, as I was saying, I've nothing to complain about as far as personal sex goes. Yet I'm sure Ron plays around a lot on the outside. Especially when I've been pregnant, and that's five times—Joe, Billie, Frank, Mary, and Larry. He's good to his family, mind you, he's a good provider—but he plays around a lot. He owns three bowling alleys, with a cocktail lounge in each one. So he's got a good excuse for staying out late, till all hours. Even though he's got a junior partner to help him check. You can imagine the women who hang around those bars. Well, anyway, he comes home once in a while smelling of perfume and also that fishy sex smell that won't come off unless you take a good shower. I guess he lays them in his office. There's a leather couch in the office of all three bowling alleys. And no shower. Just a washbasin. So he never gets rid of that perfume and sex odor."

"Does he still have sex with you?"

"You mean after laying someone else?"

"Right."

"That all depends, Graciela. If I'm pretty far along

in pregnancy, we lay off. Otherwise, we're likely to have sex even though he's been with another woman."

"He's that virile?"

"Like a bull," said Jan. "Ron has always been that way. That's why I can't stay mad at him when he's been fooling around. Wouldn't matter anyway. Whenever I mention the perfume and sweat—I mean the next morning—he says, 'I don't know what you're talking about.' Just that. Nothing more. 'I don't know what you're talking about.' He won't discuss anything, won't answer a single question."

"Sounds pretty smart to me," said Selma. "Alvin would start explaining all over the place. Complicated screwy explanations, and getting himself deeper with every word."

"Have you ever cheated on him?" asked Graciela, breaking through Selma's voice.

"Not much. Four or five times maybe. It's always with the same guy—Ron's cousin. Phil Manelli. He knows when Ron's off on one of his fishing or hunting trips and when the kids are in school. So it's always a daytime affair. Phil's a lot like Ron in bed, except that he tries to make me say dirty words while we're doing it. You know the ones I mean."

"Like fuck?"

"That and a few others. But I don't really like to say them. It makes me feel kind of whorey. And I guess that's what he wants. It excites him."

"Would your husband want you to say them?"

"Never! He'd kick me out of bed. Ron never goes for swearing from women. He's an awful strict Catholic, you know."

"Even about birth control?"

"Well, not anymore. He's pretty practical about that. After we had our five kids he realized I'd have to start wearing a diaphragm. Now it's the pills. But he's

89

told me not to tell Father Angelo. He's one of those old-fashioned Italian priests who think all women should wear black and come to church every morning. Ron was one of his altar boys a long time ago, and they've had this close relationship ever since. So you can imagine how Father Angelo would react if he knew we practiced birth control. Now, his young assistant wouldn't mind. He seems to be one of those modern priests—in the peace movement and that sort of thing—so there's no problem there. But Ron insists that I keep going to Father Angelo for confession. Says it would hurt his feelings if I switched to the younger guy."

"Feelings, crap!" snapped Graciela. "That's not his real reason, Jan. He wants you to stick to the old man because he figures you won't get into any hanky-panky you wouldn't dare to confess to Angelo. That's all."

"Could be," said Jan quietly.

"How about that business with Phil?" asked Selma. "Have you ever confessed that to Father Angelo?"

"Of course not. I went to a priest in another town. He told me to confide in my own parish priest, but I said I couldn't."

"Did he press you?"

"Oh, no—he was a pretty nice guy. He understood my position. We kinda laughed about it. I mean the cousin angle. I could see him grinning behind that thick wire mesh."

"He'll probably make a pass at you someday," said Graciela. "They've gotten pretty liberated."

"That's a terrible thing to say," Ruth protested. "You're awfully anti-Catholic."

"Priests and nuns are just human beings to me," answered Graciela. "I've seen them at fairly close range, Ruthie. There's nothing sacred about them."

"Now that you've got the floor, Graciela," said Rachel, "how about *your* sex life?"

"Well, first of all, Raul is my second husband. I was married to my high school sweetheart (God, what an old-fashioned word) for about two years before I met Raul. That first marriage to Jaime was all sex, and the second one . . . mmm . . . not much of anything—not anymore. Jaime was the first man I ever went to bed with, first one I ever seriously dated. But there was no real sex between us for a long, long time. We saw each other almost every day for nearly four years without going beyond a few hot necking sessions. He never touched my private parts or even my bare breasts. We just rubbed against each other, kissing with our lips closed and driving each other wild. But like a good little Chicana, I was saving myself for marriage. I had that old virgin crap drilled into me from the day I started menstruating. There wasn't a day that my mother didn't remind me that *solamente las mujeres decentes se casan bien,* only decent women marry well. She never got off that jazz. And my dad was probably worse. Watched me like a hawk. He was always fooling around with *putas,* like most Mexicans do, but he was bound and determined to keep me a virgin, me and my younger sister Yolanda. No matter who or when we dated (day or night), we had to take along one of our little brothers. Always some kind of chaperon."

"How did Jaime react to that?"

"He expected it, of course. He's also Mexican, so it was nothing new to him. As a matter of fact, he didn't want to screw me, not really. He wanted me to remain a virgin—to save myself for the wedding night. You can't imagine the virginity hangup most Mexicans have. If they can screw you, they won't marry you. Mom was dead right about that. She knew Jaime wouldn't marry me unless I was *decente.* So all we did was kiss and moan, kiss and moan, frustrating the hell out of each other. Except that Jaime could always relieve himself with some

91

neighborhood chippy like Lupe Borrego. *I* was the one who suffered. All I could think about was sex; it pushed everything else out of sight whenever I saw Jaime. I'd even come a few times—or masturbate when I got home. Always feeling guilty and dirty and headed for damnation. Consequently, neither Jaime nor I really got to know each other during those four years. Not until we finally got married—when we got all the sex business out of the way—not until then did I realize what a dull bastard he was. He never read anything but the sports pages. Knew nothing about literature, art, politics or anything else that interested me. We couldn't talk about a damn thing together. No matter what I mentioned— some new book I was reading, a concert, or a local political race—he'd just grunt with a blank look in his eyes or he'd change the subject to sports. Then after a while he'd say, 'What are you reading all that shit for?' Especially when I started college. . . ."

"That must have caused problems," said Trudy, breaking a momentary silence.

"It sure did. He didn't want me to get educated. But I'd gotten a full-tuition four-year scholarship to UCLA— straight A's all through high school and all that—so I wasn't about to give that up. Consequently, the more I learned, the more we drifted apart. He'd gotten a fairly good job at Sears, Roebuck and sometimes talked about night classes at this community college but didn't mean it. Sex was all we had in common, and I'll have to admit Jaime was awfully good in bed. Yet even that began to sour. He got sort of mean and tough when he screwed me. As if he were trying to prove something, trying to assert some kind of superiority. I got to feeling that his penis was a kind of weapon, something that could tear me apart inside. It was probably all in my own mind, purely subjective, but it really bothered me. Scared me. So, naturally, I started avoiding him. Made up all kinds of excuses. My vagina was irritated; I was having an abnormal discharge; my period was late. Just any damned excuse to avoid sex. So after nineteen months we agreed to split, and I moved into a dorm at the university."

"Is that where you met Raul?" asked Trudy.

"Not until my senior year. I was dating the field for a while, staying clear of any serious attachments. Most of my dates were Jewish. They seemed more interested in the things I dug—books, music, plays, the usual things. And the sex was fairly casual, a little here, a little there. No big deals. And not much pressure from any of those men. Especially the law students. I think their studies drained them. I dated three at different intervals, and they all acted impotent—distracted and impotent.

"Then I met Raul. That was at the beginning of my last year. He was a business major—one of those intense self-starting guys that you seldom find among Mexican-Americans. We didn't use the word 'Chicano' * in those days. And since there were very few of us at UCLA fifteen years ago, I guess we considered ourselves sort of special. He was particularly surprised that I'd made Phi Beta Kappa in my junior year, and I was equally impressed with his suave sure-of-himself manner and his Ivy League clothes. If ever I saw a 'comer,' it was Raul Ibañez . . . who later called himself Ralph."

"When was that?"

"About two years later. Shortly after he got his first promotion at Compton-Rex Industries. He felt that Raul was too ethnic, and he even changed the pronunciation of his last name to make it sound un-Spanish. That griped the hell out of me, and I should have divorced him right there and then. But I guess my own ambitions

* Chicano means Mexican-American or American of Mexican descent, but some Mexicans feel it's too militant—like the word "black" instead of Negro.

(middle-class security and all that) forced me to go along. We had two kids in quick session, nicely spaced so we could enjoy the bourgeois life of a typical CRI executive couple."

"I can't imagine you in that bag," said Rachel impulsively.

"Well, I'm still in it—up to my ever-loving neck. And our sex life seems just as regulated as a CRI computer: once a week the first five years, twice a month the second five years, and once a month ever since. Though I'm sure Raul is getting quite a bit of loving on the side, particularly when he's traveling. He's been the Compton-Rex man for Latin America for nearly five years, so he's down there half the time. To the *latinos* his name is Raul; then it's Ralph again as soon as he gets north of the border. He's even got two sets of calling cards: Raul Ibañez and Ralph Ibanez. So what kind of sex can you expect from that kind of man? It's cool, calculating, and passionless. But you know most of my friends think he's sexy as hell. He actually gives that impression. His dark eyes have that I-guess-you'd-call-it-suggestive look. That's why Liz, my best friend, was so surprised when I told her I'd found a new lover—ten years younger than I am. But I've been talking too much. I'll tell you about Leon some other time. It's your turn, Isabel."

Graciela's monologue was followed by rather unfocused chitchat as the second round of coffee was served. Then one of the highly sensitive hidden microphones caught Isabel's flat, nasal voice.

"I guess my sex life has a strong racial or ethnic bias. As you know, I'm Jewish, and I'm married to a WASP surgeon, a real Nordic type. Though I'm not particularly fond of Chris any more, I don't think I could ever have married a Jew. That sounds awful, I know, but let me go back to when this prejudice started. . . . Let me see. . . .

94

As I remember, the whole mess began when I was six or seven. I had this young uncle, maybe eighteen or nineteen years old (my mother's youngest brother) who came to live with us while he was in college. I was an only child, and Jeff took care of me whenever my folks went out, a most convenient live-in baby-sitter. He'd always been affectionate with me, hugging and tickling and wrestling with me the way any young father would, and my parents sort of expected that. After all, he was my uncle.

"But after a while, whenever they weren't around, Uncle Jeff got down to the real dirty business. He started fondling my thighs and fanny, making little jokes about it, then finally started to tickle my private parts—over my panties at first and then sticking his index finger under the elastic edges to feel my bare flesh, laughing all the while and pretending it was just a tickling game. And, of course, I liked it. As he knew I would. It was a tickly, exciting sensation. How could I possibly know there was anything wrong? Or even unusual? So after that I encouraged him to play with me. The minute my parents would leave the house I would start yelling, 'Let's play the tickle game, Uncle Jeff, let's play the game.' For nearly four years he played that dirty little game with me, eventually persuading me to slip off my panties and inserting his forefinger after spitting on it. 'Like doctors do,' he kept telling me. . . ."

There was a muffled sound then, perhaps the prolonged exhalation of a deep pain-remembered sigh.

"Even after he left our home, after graduating with honors and starting his doctoral studies in math, he would occasionally lure me into a bathroom and fondle me. I was nearly fourteen before he finally stopped doing it. That's when I learned that he'd been abusing me. We had a couple of lectures on child molestation at our junior high school, and it really sickened me (it was nauseating) to realize suddenly that my very own uncle, someone I loved, had done such an awful thing to me. But I wouldn't tell my folks. I didn't dare. I was afraid Dad would kill him or do something awful.

"Then when I started dating boys in high school, mostly Jewish boys from our own crowd, I couldn't help thinking they were all like my uncle. Especially if they were witty and clever and full of Jewish wisecracks. We do have a special—well, let's say a sort of *different*—culture that generally affects most of us. Consequently, they all reminded me of Uncle Jeff. Some physically. No matter how hard I reasoned with myself, I had this crazy stupid suspicion that all my Jewish dates were potential child molestors, and I would cringe and freeze whenever they so much as touched my hand. At first I thought that any male would affect me that way. But that wasn't so. When I got to college, I started dating a few gentiles and felt no repulsion when we casually held hands. In fact, I hoped they'd be intimate. Well, obviously, they didn't need much encouragement. Though I wasn't exactly an easy lay, I had relations with three or four of those eager gentiles by my senior year. That's when I met Chris, this second-year medical student whom I married a year later.

"Needless to say, my folks raised one helluva fuss, wondering why I couldn't find a nice Jewish doctor somewhere. There's got to be some available, at least one or two, Mom kept telling me. But how could I possibly tell her that her own brother had turned me away from Jews? No way. . . . Chris, of course, had the same battle with his family. Anyway, they came to the wedding with their goddamned polite smiles pasted on their Protestant faces, standing away from everyone else like a couple of frightened tourists at some damned tribal ceremony."

"Do they accept you now?"

"No. And I don't want them to. In fact, they only partially accept the kids."

"And your folks?"

"They're crazy about Linda and Little Chris. Spoil them silly. But they're still a bit cool with Big Chris. And all this family crap has obviously affected our relationship. Right after my kids were born, when I realized my in-laws would never fully accept any of us, I got this funny feeling whenever Chris and I had sex. This strange sense of betrayal—racial betrayal—would come over me. I'd suddenly freeze inside, rejecting him totally even as he was coming into me. But I don't think he sensed my reaction, at least not at the beginning. Then later on I guess he assumed that our marriage and sexual relations had simmered down to the usual indifference that occurs in most marriages. . . ."

"I'm glad you told us these things," said Ruth, suddenly breaking the brief silence. "The same thing happened to me when I was a child. Except that it was my father's best friend, who was much older than your Uncle Jeff. Probably thirty-five or so. My two brothers and I called him Uncle Billy, and he also tickled and wrestled with us. But it was different with me. He was always feeling my private parts, pretending to tickle my neck at the same time, laughing and yelling like a silly clown. It's awful to think about it, even now; yet I've never told anyone until tonight. And like Isabel, I'll have to admit that I sort of enjoyed it. I didn't know it was a dirty game until my mother warned me—several years later—never to let any strange man touch me. So I've always been suspicious of anyone where sex is concerned. I guess that's why I married Walter. He seemed safe. There was no threat from him. Just the kind of man you'd expect to meet at a church supper. But realizing how cold and distant we've always been, I've found

97

myself resenting that damned Uncle Billy for what he did to me, causing me to be so frightened of sex that I would inevitably end up with someone like Walter. What a horrible shame. I keep wondering—especially as I listened to Isabel tonight—how many thousands and thousands of little girls have been molested and psychologically messed up by uncles and family friends that no one's ever suspected. All those sick, sick men still running around playing their nasty little games. I wish now that I'd told my dad about Uncle Billy, but of course the damage had already been done when I finally caught on. It wouldn't have mattered anyway."

"Perhaps not," observed Selma. "But it might have prevented him from molesting other little girls."

"I doubt that," said Rachel. "They'd probably not take her seriously. Someone would say Ruth was exaggerating or just imagining. That's what happens in those situations. No one wants to believe the ugly truths."

"They might also think she was covering up," said Jan.

"Covering what?" asked Ruth.

"Now, I don't m-mean it that way—" said Jan, suddenly flustered. "I mean I didn't mean you, Ruth. I mean just any little girl."

"Okay, I'll accept that. But what would she be covering?"

"Well, I remember my little niece getting into something like that. She and a little boy her own age (both about seven) were playing doctor and nurse behind the garage. You know—exploring each other's privates. Then suddenly this man next door caught them and marched them right into my sister's house. But before he could say anything, my niece started screaming and accusing that man of molesting her. It was awful. A real mess. But, fortunately, my older nephew had seen the whole incident and came to his defense. That's what I meant by covering up. Little girls do that sort of thing. So, having heard my own niece falsely accusing someone, I'd be very skeptical if *my* daughter accused someone."

"Maybe, maybe not," said Selma. "I used to play doctor and nurse with my little cousin (now a famous gynecologist, mind you), but I don't think I would have accused anyone else. But, of course, Irving and I never got caught, so what can I tell you?"

"Now that we're talking about all these sexual traumas," said Trudy, clearing her voice in mid-sentence, "do any of you remember the very first time you went all the way with a man?"

"Of course!" said a chorus of voices.

"It would take me a full hour to tell you about mine," said Rachel. "But I don't think we've got time for any more confessions tonight. It's almost midnight."

"I'm afraid she's right," said Selma. "Time to fold. We'll talk about our farewells to virginity in our session dealing with childhood and adolescence."

"I can barely wait," said Trudy.

V

Intermission

JOHN had always assumed that his wife was quite fond of him, that their marriage was among the happier, more successful ones in Westlake. Consequently he was angered and disillusioned by some of his wife's disparaging comments during the first three secretly taped meetings and was sorely tempted to confront her with the tapes and to accuse her of being devious and two-faced. But he was soon dissuaded by his innately cautious attorney.

"You're in a helluva position to claim duplicity," the lawyer had told him. "No matter what reasons you give for bugging those rap sessions. That was a crappy thing to do."

"It started as a joke," John tried to explain. "I got so goddamned curious, particularly with that sudden change in her attitude toward me—all that business about my being a latent chauvinist pig. I mean, what the fuck did she mean by *latent?*"

"That still doesn't justify your spying on her conversations with other women, John. That could be grounds for divorce, and it would screw up the works just now."

"How so?"

"Well, as you damned well know, she'd be entitled to half your total assets under community property law. And any litigation would blow that merger you've been planning."

"I see your point, Herb. I'll cool it."

Having thus prevented John from taking any pre-cipitous action, the lawyer subsequently heard the first few tapes and was quickly convinced they could provide the basis for a valuable book or manual on marital relations. Meanwhile—in fact, just a few days after that initial consultation with his attorney—John had a long talk with his wife about Women's Lib, hoping she might eventually allude to her own consciousness-raising group. Since he had already decided to continue taping the weekly rap sessions for the book Herb had suggested, he also recorded this particular conversation.

"What are you gals talking about these days?" he asked offhandedly after a few preliminary remarks about a Susskind show featuring four ardent feminists.

"We no longer accept that term, John."

"What term?"

"*Gals.* We think it's derogatory and demeaning."

"Jesus—I didn't mean it to be."

"Well, as far as we're concerned, it's in the same category as 'dames' and 'broads.' "

"Okay, I stand corrected. Now may I respectfully ask what you—"

"No need for sarcasm, John."

"Okay, I didn't mean to be. But I'd sure like to know what you women are talking about these days?"

"Our rap group?"

"Right."

"Well, I can't tell you, John."

"Not even in general, abstract terms? I'm not asking for specific details."

"But we don't talk in general terms or abstractions. We talk only about very specific and quite personal things. Which we're not supposed to discuss with anyone outside the group."

"Well, let me put it this way: Are you talking about

politics, sex, children, lesbianism, mother complexes, divorce, or anything like that?"

"Yes, we're talking about most of the topics you've mentioned, but always in very personal terms. And it's really kind of exciting to talk about such things as sex, motherhood, and children on a very personal this-is-what-I-feel or this-is-what-I-do level of consciousness."

"I'm not sure I get you," said John.

"Okay, I'll say it this way: We always (or should always) talk in the first person. Like 'I can't stand my husband's hairy shoulders' or something like 'I'm sure my orgasms are clitoral rather than vaginal.' That sort of personal awareness and candor."

"Do all of you get that personal?"

"Some more than others," she answered with an ambiguous smile. "Two or three of our members would shock almost anyone, even Norman Mailer."

"So when it comes to sex, you really get down to the nitty-gritty?"

"We get to the nitty-gritty on everything, John. Sex isn't our only concern. Though it's certainly damned important."

"And you?" he asked, recalling how shocked he'd been when he heard her recorded voice calling him a bum lay. "Are you that candid?"

"Sometimes. Though I'm not as graphic as some of the others. But I'm getting there, John."

"I can well imagine," he said, instantly regretting the irony in his voice.

"What is *that* supposed to mean?"

"Nothing, nothing at all. Just an offhand remark."

"There's no such thing as an *offhand remark*," she insisted. "Particularly in that tone of voice."

(John later told me how uncomfortable he felt at that moment, inwardly squirming and wondering if she had somehow sensed that he knew more than he should about their rap sessions. But he managed, or *hoped* he had managed, to muffle his secret guilt by a not-too-subtle diversion to another aspect of the recent tension between them.)

"Well, to tell you the truth," he said, looking toward the bookcase to avoid her stare, "I've been wondering—worrying actually—about how much you've changed these past few weeks. Since those meetings began."

"I should hope so," she said. "That's what consciousness raising is all about. We're supposed to change."

"I know that, Pooch. But, Jesus Christ, you're becoming completely antimale. There must be some of us who aren't male chauvinist pigs!"

"Very few, John. Damned few. And, incidentally, I don't want you to call me Pooch anymore."

"Oh. Why not?"

"Because it's one of those stupid little nicknames that men use as a subtle put-down. Most of them are pretty damned insulting when you really analyze them. Take *Pooch*, for example, it's—"

"I know what you're going to say," said John, breaking in.

"Of course you do. Because Pooch is so obviously a cute way of saying 'bitch.' "

"So now you're going to tell me that I've subconsciously been calling you a bitch for the last fifteen years. Except that your own father called you Pooch before I ever met you. That's where I got the goddamned name! So don't lay that chauvinist crap on me."

She smiled at first, then burst into a fit of laughter that nearly gagged her. And when she started to say something about her father, another spasm of laughter cut her short. Finally, controlling herself as John handed her a glass of water from the bar, she managed to explain why she had reacted so wildly to what he had said.

"You certainly got me on that one," she said. "But there's something even funnier about that name. My father's younger sister was called Pooch. So was my grandmother. And even my great-grandmother was called Pooch. So I come from a long line of bitches—at least four generations. . . . Wait till I tell the girls about *that* one."

"What girls?"

"The ones in our group."

"I thought they were *women*."

"Okay, John, you've got me again. It's just as bad for me to say 'girls' as it is for you to say it. But that just goes to show you how we've all been victimized—men just as much as women—by old language patterns that continually put down women."

"Well, I'm glad you're willing to concede that we're *all* victimized. You know, it's awfully damned hard to restructure your whole damned vocabulary overnight. But, damn it, I'm trying. As a matter of fact, it's already costing me quite a bit."

"How so?"

"In my company's mailing lists," he said. "I've ordered thousands of new name plates for all the women in our customer and prospective-customer files. All of them will be *Ms.* from now on."

"Hey, that's great. I'll tell the girls—I m-mean the group."

"Just good business," he said, a touch embarrassed by the unexpected praise.

"That lowers your chauvinist rating by one point," she added before his ego could reach the bursting stage.

"What rating?" he asked.

"Well, I'm not supposed to tell anyone," she said, with no visible sign of self-restraint. "But each one of us has rated our husband on a male-chauvinist scale that

104

goes from one to ten, with the least *macho* rated number one."

"Scales usually start at zero, my love."

"We know that, John. But we've unanimously agreed that no man can achieve the zero ideal. And damned few can get below five."

"And what's my rating?"

"That, my dear John, you'll never know. I've already told you more than I should."

"Am I lower than Frank Sinatra?"

"Everyone is. We'd rate him ninety-nine-plus, the total chauvinist pig."

"How about Nixon?"

"You'd have to ask Pat. And she'd probably have to ask Bebe Rebozo."

"How about McGovern?"

"He's either a five or a ten, depending on what group he's trying to con. But I personally think he's closer to ten, no matter what Shirley MacLaine keeps telling us. I'll vote for him anyway."

The infinite possibilities of such ratings had an instant appeal for John.

"This could be a damned interesting gimmick for a cocktail party," he mused audibly. "You would get each woman to rate her husband from one to ten, toss their slips into a hat, then the hostess or host would draw a slip, read the man's name, and ask everyone to guess the number."

"And you'd have ten divorces after every party," she added. "Unless they all lied."

"Would you lie?"

"Probably. Particularly at some stupid party, where you'd get nothing but snickering locker-room jokes about things most people are afraid to discuss seriously."

"But it would just be a game," he protested.

105

"Not with us, it isn't. Those ratings are a serious matter, John. And I'd prefer not to talk about them anymore. And please, please don't mention them to anyone. I shouldn't have told you."

"Okay, Pooch. Mum's the word," he promised. "And please forgive me for calling you Pooch again. Hard to drop an old habit."

"That's all right. You can still call me Pooch. But not in front of the girls—I mean the w-women."

VI

Early Childhood

Women have been taught to fear freedom and to shun it when by chance it comes their way.

—LUCINDA CISLER,
Sisterhood Is Powerful

BECAUSE of a heavy rainstorm which delayed three of the women, the fourth session got under way about twenty minutes beyond the usual hour. And when they finally began their discussion, after a few preliminary remarks about a regional meeting of NOW (National Organization of Women), Isabel startled most of them by announcing that she probably wouldn't be coming to any more meetings.

"My husband has gotten awfully upset about my new attitudes," she said with more sadness than rancor. "And he's asked me not to come anymore. I guess he suspects there's something very mysterious—maybe sinister—going on at these sessions. Especially since I refuse to tell him what we talk about."

"He feels threatened," said Graciela. "Raul feels the same way. He tries to joke about it, but I can tell that it's really resentment."

"That's to be expected," Trudy added offhandedly. "How would *we* feel if they were meeting every week and refusing to tell us anything?"

"How about their damned poker nights?"

"They're different," said Isabel, regaining the floor. "We know they're actually playing poker and probably telling a few dirty jokes. But I seriously doubt they ever have any deep-down discussions about themselves or their marriages, except for the usual cracks about bitchy wives, et cetera. But nothing as frank as our talks."

"That's right," agreed Selma. "They'd never level with each other about personal problems the way women do. Alvin has always admitted that."

"Anyway," said Isabel. "Getting back to my original point about not coming to any more meetings, I just wanted to—well, sort of explain that I'm terribly ambivalent about all this. I've been worrying all day, deciding to quit at midmorning, then changing my mind at noon. Going back and forth with each cup of black coffee, and finally calling Selma after my fifth change of mind. . . ."

"Then she almost changed *my* mind," Selma interrupted with a mock sigh in her voice.

"You were only pretending," continued Isabel. "You didn't want to pressure me. And you were right when you told me it had to be my own personal decision—that you'd understand either way."

"Well, I'm glad you came, Isabel. At least one more time. We need you, sweetie. We all need each other."

"I'm the one who needs you, and I certainly don't want to quit. . . . But my husband came home as I was leaving tonight, and he got this awful hurt look in his face when he realized where I was going. His mouth tightened, kind of trembled, and his eyes stared right past me. 'So you're going again,' he mumbled. As if I were going off to see some secret lover. Well, I didn't say anything, I just left. But it made me feel terribly guilty and disloyal. . . .

"You've got to understand how different this is for

us. We've never gone off on our own like this before. I'm not saying we've had a close relationship, because we haven't. There's always been a distance between us. A not being really together. But that—well, let's call it alienation—has always been internal. On the surface we've had this phony togetherness. Now, however, even the kids have noticed it. Just last week I heard one of them asking, 'Where's mom going, dad—all by herself at night?'"

"What was his answer?"

"I don't know, Rachel. He mumbled something. Or shrugged his shoulders as if he didn't know. So the next morning I explained to both of them that I would always be attending a strictly female meeting every Thursday night. That, and nothing more."

"Maybe we're being too mysterious," said Rachel. "I see no harm in telling our husbands and kids that we're discussing our roles and status as women. We don't have to be too explicit. We can generalize."

"I think you're right," agreed Trudy. "We must seem sort of paranoid (or a bit juvenile) with all this closed-mouth business. I think we should loosen up. As a matter of fact, I've already told John what we talk about—*but in very general terms.* Just this morning, while we were having coffee, I told him that tonight we'd be discussing our childhood. And that was enough."

"Let's all loosen up with our menfolk. And now that you've mentioned *childhood,* why don't we get on with our business?" said Rachel.

"Fine, Rachel. We'll start with you."

"Well, speaking as a black woman, I guess my early childhood was fairly ordinary. I was daddy's little girl and mommy's little helper. Spoiled silly by everyone— even my brothers, three of them older than me. All I had to do was cry a little bit, and they'd come running to take care of me. But if any of my brothers cried, especially

THE SEVEN WIVES OF WESTLAKE

when dad was around, they'd catch hell. Boys weren't allowed to cry. . . ."

"Isn't that the truth?" said Graciela, breaking in. "They're all supposed to be *machos,* even as little kids."

"And that's rather sad," Rachel continued. "They can't cry or show any weakness. They're forced into a phony he-man role when they're mere children. So how can they possibly mature if they can't go through that process of showing emotion or weakness and then coping with it?"

"That's an interesting notion, Rachel. I've never thought of it that way."

"Neither did I until my own son was growing up. His dad—that's my first husband—was a demon on that score. He couldn't stand to see boys cry. That made 'em sissies in his book."

"And that's so tragic," Selma added. "Having to hold back tears and not showing what they feel. That male mask of *machismo* hiding all those little-boy fears and hurts. All those emotions bottled up year after year until they finally burst—either inside with ulcers or outside with raging anger."

"Or heart attacks," mumbled someone.

"That's why males won't ever have rap sessions like these," said Trudy somewhat wistfully. "I guess most of them have lost the ability to admit weakness and fear. John certainly has. He often gets a worried look on his face, but he'll never tell me what it's about. Never."

"And we go to the other extreme," observed Ruth. "We let it all out—with tears and the whole works."

"That comes from early training," said Rachel, not quite repressing a chuckle. "I learned about the power of tears before I could crawl and kept getting more expert at it year after year. But it was mostly soft whimpering with me—none of that earsplitting angry stuff that just annoyed people. I played it soft. With plenty of big tears.

110

And let me tell you how well it worked: My daddy always carried this picture of me in his wallet (carried it for years), and there I was with these big tears running down my cheeks and my mouth ready to pout. That's what really got to him, those tears. So I played that role right to the hilt. Daddy's helpless little girl. Of course I smiled a great deal—but only for contrast. . . ."

"You must have been a born actress, Rachel."

"Well, now that you mention it, I've got to confess that crying was my main forte when I finally became a professional actress. In fact, my only forte. I've always been able to gush a flood of tears at the snap of a finger. And that's awfully important when you've got a two-minute part in one of those television soap operas. Any actress can pretend to sob, but damn few of us can produce real tears for a tight shooting schedule."

"Did you ever cry for real?" someone asked.

"When?"

"When you were a little girl."

"Oh, lots of times. But I particularly remember a summer afternoon when we were up in the mountains on a family picnic. My father was teaching my brothers how to fish for trout, tossing out the line with this fluid motion and reeling it in again. It looked so easy and beautiful I wanted to try it, too. But daddy kept saying, 'This is for boys,' and wouldn't let me. 'Go pick flowers with your mommy,' he told me. 'And help her fix the sandwiches.' So I sat there at the picnic table, jealously watching my brothers and smearing too much mayonnaise on everything. I guess it was the closeness between my brothers and my father that hurt me most, seeing them huddled together baiting the hooks and laughing and having that male intimacy I've always envied. Whenever I see men fishing together or playing poker or just drinking in some bar, I suddenly remember that afternoon. I guess that was the first time I ever felt excluded from my father's

111

world, my very first consciousness of sexual separation."

"But don't you think little boys feel the same way when they see mother and daughter baking a pie together or fixing a hem?"

"I doubt it, Ruth. I really do. I've never seen any little boy raising hell because he's been excluded from the kitchen or some other female thing."

"Maybe they do, but are afraid to express it for fear of being called a sissy."

"Could be, Ruth, but I seriously doubt it. After all, it's the so-called male things that are considered adventurous and romantic—like hunting and fishing and all kinds of sports. So they've made us the weaker sex by excluding us from anything that requires a little muscle."

"But that's how we're built. There's no sense denying that."

"I'm not so sure," Rachel snapped back. "I could outwrestle and outrun any boy in my second-grade class. The only one tougher than me was Sally Burton . . . but she finally became a sissy in the fourth grade, a brainy little sissy who got straight A's all through elementary and junior high school. Then she suddenly got dumb and sexy in the tenth grade."

"That's what happened to me." It was Isabel's voice, flat and more nasal than usual. "I was one of those so-called whiz kids, a compulsive reader. I even read all the print on cereal boxes. Consequently, I was always way ahead in our reading assignments, finishing the damned books while everyone else was on chapter one. No—that's not really so. There were four or five other kids pretty far ahead, three girls and two boys. But as a group, the girls were generally better students than the boys."

"Same at my school," said Trudy and Graciela.

"That's a general pattern," Selma added. "Little girls are always ahead till they develop breasts and become sexpots. All that brain fluid sinks to their boobies. Any scientist knows that."

"But it was my mother who pushed the get-sexy bit," said Isabel. "For years, right up until my fifteenth birthday, both my parents encouraged me to become a brain. Even that sex-maniac young uncle of mine—my mother's brother—joined the act by teaching me to play chess and reading poetry to me. Then suddenly my dear Jewish mommy got worried about my round shoulders. 'Stop reading so much,' she kept telling me. 'You'll end up a hunchback, a nearsighted hunchback like that fella who plays for Notre Dame.' That was her favorite little joke in those days, and she repeated it at least once a week. But she wasn't kidding about my becoming round-shouldered. That worried hell out of her. 'Nobody cares what a man looks like as long as he's got a profession or some money,' she warned me. 'But who wants a hunchback girl who reads too much? You've got to be attractive, Isabel, if you expect to be married.'

"She'd go on like that every day, sometimes forcing dad to join her campaign. 'But I'm only fifteen,' I'd tell them. 'It's too early to think about marriage.' Not for her it wasn't. She was worried about my shoulders and my eyes and my getting so brainy I'd scare off the potential husband she carried around in her imagination, that perfect young doctor or lawyer or millionaire business-man that all mothers dream their daughters should marry."

"All *Jewish* mothers," said Trudy. "Like mine."

"*All* mothers," said Ruth. "Including us WASP's."

"And Catholics, too," Jan chimed in. "Except that we don't joke about it. Jewish mothers are more famous because there are more Jewish comedians and novelists. I could introduce you to a hundred Portnoy's mothers in any Italian neighborhood."

"Okay—so all mothers are alike."

113

"*Most* mothers," protested Rachel. "There must be some who are slightly different. In all ethnic groups."

"I wish I were different," said Selma. "I feel myself falling into the same mother trap. Already I'm pressuring my daughter, Shari, with all that catch-a-man crap. It's like teaching her to be a married hustler—all the same little tricks my mother taught me."

"Hey there!" someone blurted. "You've read the same book I've just been reading."

"Which book?"

"This one, Selma. It's called *Sisterhood Is Powerful.* I brought it tonight because I wanted to read you all a couple of passages that deal exactly on what we're talking about. Listen to this on page two hundred and ninety, from an essay written by an ex-prostitute:

> From the time a girl is old enough to go to school, she begins her education in the basic principles of hustling. Now there is certainly some conflict there, because on the one hand she is being taught, verbally, to value love, self-worth, pride, compassion, and humanness, while on the other hand she is receiving distinct messages from those around her (from parents on down through her favorite television personalities) that the really important goals are economic ascendancy and status acquisition; and that she, a female, can acquire all these things if she plays her hand right. So, in reality, all the hustler has done is to eliminate the flowery speeches and put things where they're really at. Without the games, she will trade what is regarded as a commodity anyway, for what she wants. . . .

"And there's a lot more, but you get the—"

"Go ahead and read it, Trudy. At least finish the paragraph."

"Well, okay. Here it is:

> . . . and if you doubt that sex is regarded as a commodity by more than just those who patronize the

114

hustler, listen to any conversation among a group of men when they get together, and hear the way they discuss women. There still exists a widespread belief that a woman is little more than a receptacle for some man's "come." The most painful thing about that particular attitude is that many women believe it as well. Rather than sharing love and sex, we have been taught to use it.

There was a brief silence when she'd finished reading the passage; then Jan came forth with the first reaction. "She may have a point, but she's taken it too far. There's a big difference between a wife and a whore. After all, a wife isn't selling herself to just anyone."

"Just her husband," said Rachel. "Especially if she no longer loves him."

"Oh, come on!" protested Ruth. "There's a difference in *attitude*. I don't feel like a whore just because I let my husband support me. I damn well earn that support—even if I never go to bed with him."

"Then what's the point of staying with him?"

"Because, quite frankly, I'd be afraid to get a divorce at this stage of the game. But I still don't feel like a prostitute."

"You're right, Ruthie," said Selma, suddenly breaking in as if to forestall a potential argument. "That gal sounds as if she's rationalizing for having been a hooker. Yet there's an element of truth in what she says. I guess there's a bit of hustler in almost any woman, including some very famous ones."

"I know just who you mean," someone chortled in the background. "But she's in a class all by herself."

"I wonder who taught *her*," Isabel mused out loud. "She really learned to score big, as the hustlers say."

"Well, it wasn't her mama," said Rachel with blunt assurance. "Understand she was a real daddy's girl when she was growing up."

115

"Weren't we all?" asked Graciela. "I certainly was, I worshiped my dad from the minute I was born. Right up until he died a couple of years ago. He used to take me everywhere when I was growing up. He even taught me how to fish, Rachel. That's why I smiled when you were telling us that your dad thought fishing was only for boys. I guess my father made a tomboy out of me. There was nothing he wouldn't do for me, including most of my math homework. So, as you might expect, I developed this awful crush on him. Which eventually caused a lot of problems with my mother, the problems some of us are experiencing with our own daughters."

"You can say that again," said Selma.

"And my daddy crush got particularly bad when I was around thirteen or fourteen. I would actually dream—not once, but many times—that my mom had died or simply gone away, so that I could take her place. Sometimes I'd even tell her to stay in bed, that *I* would cook dad's breakfast and get him off to work. But she soon put a stop to that. She'd get up no matter how tired or lazy she felt. That didn't stop me, however. Not on your life. I'd still get up and make his toast and fix fresh orange juice while mom made coffee and fried the eggs and sausage."

"He sure must have loved that," said Isabel. "Two women fighting over him and spoiling him to death. A real *macho's* paradise."

"How about your husband, Raul?" asked Ruth. "Do you and Erlinda spoil him?"

"Not with the breakfast bit. She's a lot lazier than I was, and so am I. He's got to boil his own water for Nescafé and pour his own juice while we both stay in bed."

There was approving laughter from most of the seven wives, and someone cheered with a couple of "right

116

ons," after which Ruth managed to catch their attention with her crisp, well-controlled voice.

"While we're on the subject of wanting to take mother's place, I distinctly remember always jumping into the front seat of the car next to my father and asking mother to sit in the back. But I never realized until I got to college—when I took a psych course—that my motives were sort of sexual, and I got into a terrible argument with this young professor. To be perfectly honest, his explanation still bothers me, although it does seem pretty logical. I'd rather think it was just ordinary daughterly affection."

"That's all it was," said Jan quite emphatically. "All this Freudian stuff seems pretty sick to me. Nothing seems to be free of sex to some people, and I get pretty damned tired of it all."

"So do I, Jan—and I'm a psychologist." It was Selma's voice cutting through several others that sympathized with Jan. "There's a lot of Freudian psychology that's no longer accepted. He was a sexist—a product of his own *macho* environment—but we can't ignore everything he said."

"Do you believe all the Oedipus stuff—about most boys having sexual hangups with their mothers?" someone asked.

"Some of it, Ruth. But that theory was developed at least two thousand years before Freud was born. He just gave it a clinical slant."

"It still nauseates me."

"That's because we—I mean society in general—tend to moralize too much about natural functions. . . ."

"Watch it, Selma," warned Trudy. "We're getting too analytical."

"You're right. I'm sorry. Now let me be specific

about myself. I also had a crush on my father, and it wasn't strictly platonic or little-girlish. But that was nothing compared to the crush I had later on, the one I had on my brother. And of course I couldn't tell anyone. But no one. I had to keep it all bottled up inside, hating every girl he ever dated . . . and spying on them whenever I could. God, I was screwed up! No wonder I became a psychologist. So you see, Ruthie, I can't exactly pooh-pooh all that stuff Freud wrote about."

"I'm sure glad you've admitted all that," said Graciela. "Because I had the same kind of thing with my brother. I absolutely hated his girlfriends; and sometimes—when my breasts were just beginning to develop —I'd walk around in this flimsy see-through blouse, trying to grab his attention with a silly sexy strut that I'm embarrassed to remember. . . . Then one afternoon when our high school was having a beach party (I was a sophomore and my brother was a senior), I started menstruating and he took me aside and told me I had blood on my white bikini. Whispered it so no one else could hear. Well, I managed to get some Tampax and changed into my jeans; but I couldn't face him for at least a week. My own brother! And there I was—so damned embarrassed because he knew I'd been menstruating. . . ."

"That's how I felt about my period—embarrassed and almost ashamed," Ruth confided in a shy voice. "I didn't want even my closest girlfriends to know. But of course they could always tell. I'd go around with this pained look in my face, those darned cramps tearing me apart for three or four days, making me feel that I really had been cursed. As a matter of fact, that darned Methodist mother of mine frequently hinted that I was being punished for something. 'God has his ways,' she'd say. 'None of us escapes what's due.' That's all the comfort I'd get from her."

118

"She sounds pretty religious."

"Well, 'churchy' would be a better word. Our whole darned family was *churchy* rather than truly religious. In fact, going to church was about our only social activity when I was growing up. Church suppers, church socials, church picnics, church Bible schools, church everything. Our entire lives revolved around that drab First Methodist Church and the community center attached to it. How I envied the Catholics I knew, with their big fancy church and their noisy dances at St. Mary's School, which my parents considered the most wicked thing they could imagine, particularly when they had bingo games on the side."

"When did you finally leave all that?"

"Well, that's the terrible part: I never did until the fourth or fifth year of my marriage. As I've said before, I met Walter at a church supper when I came home for Easter during my last year in college. His uncle was a visiting pastor, a classmate of our pastor. So as you can obviously see, I had a rather restricted childhood. I didn't even know enough to have evil thoughts."

"That's all I *ever* had when I was young—evil thoughts. Especially when I got to be a teen-ager." Trudy again, her well-modulated voice now tinged with irony. "I'd squirm inside every time a boy came near me. But that was all on the inside. On the outside I would put on this bored, indifferent act, this sad little pretense to cover my fear of rejection because of the awful acne on my chin. No boy—certainly none that appealed to me—would ask for a date or even talk to me. So I'd snub them before they could snub me. Then I'd go home to lie in bed and imagine myself necking like mad with every boy I had pretended to snub, lying there alone with tears in my eyes, trying my best not to play with myself and turning my radio on as loud as possible.

"I must have used a whole jar of Noxsema every

119

week trying to get rid of that damned acne. The more I worried, the worse it got, and the worse it got, the more I'd worry. Meanwhile, this beautiful clear-skinned friend of mine, Jill Kendig, was dating the entire football team (or so it seemed), and she'd occasionally get me a blind date. So there I'd go—four-eyed, chin-scarred, my palms sweating, yet pretending to be bored and totally unavailable, when in fact, every one of those pimply-faced guys could have rolled me into the hay with a mere flick of the wrist. I was dying to get mauled by just anyone."

"Did you?"

"Just once, Rachel. That was Jeff Wolman, this big clumsy second-string tackle, whose hands were sweatier than mine and whose acne was a lot worse. So we got into this incredibly awkward what-do-I-do-next necking match in the back seat of his buddy's Buick. I could feel his huge hands searching for the zipper on my blouse as he bruised my half-open mouth with his chapped lips, and his fat right knee pushing against my crotch as if I were an opposing tackle he had to block out of the way."

"Jesus! What a wonderful scene that would make," cried Rachel through a medley of giggles. "For a movie, I mean. Some sort of comedy about high school kids."

"Well, it sounds pretty funny now," conceded Trudy. "But it certainly wasn't funny when it happened. It was a total fiasco for both of us. And believe it or not, I kinda felt sorry for Jeff. He ended up apologizing with an awful stutter, telling me, 'I ain't very good at this sorta thing. I start sweating too much and I get this wild feeling inside that drives me crazy, like I'm going to bust open.' Then after a while, after stuttering one apology after another, he finally said, 'I don't see how anybody can stand an ugly pug like me.' And that's when I started crying. I just couldn't help myself. He was so miserable and pathetic and down on himself. Then he started crying with me. But mostly inside himself, with his mouth clamped tight and his huge chest heaving with held-in sobs. So I put my arms around him and held him close, mumbling these crazy words that didn't make sense. I wanted to tell him how ugly and lonely I felt, but I just couldn't bring myself to admit it—as if admitting it would somehow destroy me. . . ."

"But you must have been beautiful (you still are)," protested Ruth. "So a little acne can't make you ugly, Trudy."

"It can if you're the one who has it, Ruth. Believe me. It can make you feel ugly as hell."

"I can certainly believe you," said Jan. "I had acne for about a year. On my forehead. You can still see the little scars and blotches when I don't cover them with makeup."

"My problem was pimples and oily skin." It was Graciela breaking in with a reminiscent sigh in her voice. "All through high school—pimply face and excess fat. Stuffing myself with pizzas, french fries, chocolate malts and peanut butter sandwiches while I sat cross-legged on my fat haunches listening to Anita O'Day and Billie Holiday records and doing my homework or writing long letters to—"

"That sure sounds like my daughter, Shari," observed Selma distractedly. "Except for the singers' names. It's all rock for her."

"Every weekend I'd promise myself—and my ever-worrying *mamacita*—to go on a diet she'd found in the *Reader's Digest*. But by Tuesday afternoon I'd be sneaking off to the pizza parlor. And sometimes I'd reward myself with a combination Mexican dinner—*taco, enchilada, tamale* and *frijoles refritos*—exactly thirty thousand, one hundred and seventy-eight calories in every serving. So I'd eat only half the *frijoles* and reduce it to twenty-seven thousand, four hundred and seven calories. My only salvation was that my Chicano boyfriend, that hypocrite *macho* who helped preserve my virginity against my will, was almost as fat as I was. He also realized that I was a hot necker in spite of my pimply face."

"That's hard to believe, Graciela."

"That I was a hot necker?"

"No, not that," said Isabel. "I meant that it's hard to believe that your fantastically smooth skin has ever had a single pimple."

"I've got a few pictures to prove it. Which also show the fat I was talking about. But, fortunately, my photo in the yearbook shows me as clear-skinned as I am today. Those damned pimples disappeared in the middle of my senior year."

"That's a strange coincidence," said Trudy. "My acne disappeared in my senior year—but completely. Suddenly I was beautiful. Or at least attractive. I started dating like mad. As if to make up for all those years of staying at home when everybody else was going out. I started dating a different boy every night, almost anyone who asked me, including my best friend's favorite boyfriend. Until my dad—poor worried dad—took me on a long walk one evening and gave me that inevitable spiel about boy-crazy girls losing everyone's respect. He sounded so stern and old-fashioned. And also a bit melancholy, perhaps because he basically understood and empathized with my sudden hunger for male attention. So I gradually tapered off and got a bit more choosy . . . and less frantic."

There was a long pause after she'd finished, as if all seven women were suddenly remembering their own teen-age longings and frustrations, inwardly focusing on some long-ago episode that had been heartbreakingly poignant or unforgettably amusing. It was Jan who finally broke the silence.

"I'm so glad we've talked about all these things, about how we really felt as teen-agers or even younger.

Right now, I'm beginning to see my own kids in a different light."

"Same here," Isabel agreed. "I guess I'll be a little more understanding with Linda. For a while at least. Until she calls me a bitch again."

"In my case, that will be tomorrow," said Selma with a heavy sigh. "Shari calls me a bitch or a witch at least twice every morning before she runs off for the school bus. In the summertime she doesn't call me a bitch until noon—because she doesn't get up until then. But you're right, Ruthie, these sessions are making me understand all of them a little better. Even my husband. Especially my husband."

"Why your husband especially?"

"Wellll . . . well, let me put it this way, Ruth. As I've been listening to what we've said about little boys and all the pressure they get to act like he-men, I'm more acutely aware of how Alvin's been victimized by the same *macho* code. Then as we were talking about our fathers refereeing spats between menopause mama and menstruating daughter, I can easily visualize my husband in exactly the same role, which ain't a bowl of cherries for anybody—including, you should excuse the reference, Jesus Christ."

"You're right," said Rachel. "Our menfolk *do* have a hard row to hoe (especially if they're black), but we've got a *harder* row. And it's full of the crap they've left behind. So let's not get *too* understanding, sweetie."

"About me, you don't have to worry, Rachel. I'm the original *kvetch numero uno,* if you'll accept a mixed-ethnic metaphor. . . . Now how about a little coffee or tea?"

"Okay, Selma—but when are we going to talk about the most crucial part of our childhood or girlhood— whatever you want to call it?"

"And what would that be?"

"Our first sexual experience."

"Ah, yes . . . of course. . . . But let's have some coffee first. We may need it."

During the brief intermission there was considerable laughter from the far side of the room (away from the three hidden microphones), where the coffee percolator was perched on the bar. One can only assume that either Selma or Rachel, the most persistent humorists in the group, had told another of their apparently vast store of jokes about male chauvinists. When the seven wives returned to the discussion area around the large coffee table, the first voice coming into clear focus was Isabel's:

". . . but I've already told you about my first sex experience—that sickening business with my young uncle, my mother's favorite little brother."

"That doesn't count, Isabel. We're talking about the more or less normal stuff between boys and girls in junior or senior high school."

"Well, if that's what you mean, I'll have to tell you about Lloyd Walzer and Sandy Baron. . . ."

"Three of you?"

"No, it's not what you're thinking, Trudy. Not at all." A hint of impatience in her voice. "It happened in the ninth grade. The three of us—Lloyd, Sandy, and I—were in this play together, some dumb one-act comedy about the son trying to get the family car for a Saturday-night date with his girlfriend—me. Anyway, there were some people (mostly our parents and relatives) who thought we'd been pretty funny and cute, so the three of us went out to celebrate after the final performance. At this roadhouse. But, of course, they wouldn't let us in. So Lloyd sneaked into his house and got a bottle of vodka from his dad's liquor cabinet, and we went back to this grassy area behind the school library to have a few drinks—vodka and root beer. . . ."

"You've got to be kidding."

124

"No—that's all we could get. And it really tasted okay. Well, anyway, they both got horny and silly and immediately started to grab at my breasts and thighs and taking turns kissing me with their slobbery mouths. Then Sandy got a little bolder and worked his hand under my panties, getting me excited as a cat in heat—a really wild feeling. Then Lloyd suddenly walked off and left me alone with Sandy, pretending he had to take a pee somewhere. So by this time Sandy and I were necking and rubbing into each other like mad. When suddenly he jerked himself into a half-sitting position and vomited all over me—threw up everything he'd eaten since breakfast, right on this new dress I'd gotten just for the play. Can you possibly imag—"

Rumbles of laughter drowned her voice before she could finish the question, and she herself joined in the rib-splitting laughter, her voice still choking as she added, "And that was my sexual baptism!"

"Ain't nobody gonna top that one," predicted Rachel. "But tell us, Isabel, whatever happened to Sandy?"

"Now you may not believe this, Rachel—but Sandy finally settled down and became a very conservative rabbi."

"Orthodox or Reform?"

"That I can't tell you. Someone told me a few years ago that he's connected with a synagogue somewhere in the East, but she couldn't remember anything else."

"And you never dated him after that episode?"

"Oh, no. He couldn't even look at me. And neither could Lloyd for some screwy reason."

"Maybe you still smelled of vomit," said Selma. "That doesn't go away easy."

Much laughter again; then someone asked Graciela to tell her story.

"I've already mentioned my first experience, and it came pretty late. I was a typical Chicana virgin until I married my first husband."

"What about your first—your very first—experience with him? I mean before you actually went to bed with him."

"Well, as I said before, there was an awful lot of hot necking with him. But the first really sexy session occurred when I was around the tenth grade, the early part. We were on the back porch near midnight, and Jaime had sort of cornered me between the broom cabinet and this old refrigerator that my dad used as a tool chest. Having gradually moved me into that wedge, he had pushed one knee between my legs and was trying to pry my lips open with his tongue to give me a French kiss, and I had closed my mouth so tight my jaws were aching. But God, how I wanted him. Not only to kiss me the way he wanted, but to go all the way. Yet my damned old virginity complex wouldn't yield. So I kept my lips sealed tight as a drum, my heart thumping like thunder as his slobbery lips and tongue probed more and more. Finally, to relieve the pressure on my jaw muscles, I opened my mouth slightly and his hard pointed tongue slid between my teeth; but he suddenly jerked away from me, his mouth reddened with blood. He'd cut his tongue on my front teeth. Two big gashes. . . ."

"How awful!"

"It sure was, Ruth."

"What did you do?"

"Well, he ran home holding his handkerchief over his mouth, and his dad got him to an emergency hospital."

"And you?"

"I got hell for ruining my new white blouse. His blood had splattered my collar and one sleeve. So I told them Jaime had gotten a nosebleed. But a week later

Jaime's dad told my dad that Jaime had cut his tongue, and I got a second bawling out, an awful two-hour fit of *macho* rage. You'd think that I'd lost my virginity to Jaime and his whole damned family."

"Did Jaime catch hell from his father?"

"Not on your life!" snapped Graciela. "He told me his dad laughed like hell about it and merely advised him to be more careful the next time."

"That figures," said Trudy with an edge of bitterness in her voice. "He gets praised for being a lecher, and you catch hell for being the victim."

"But there was some poetic justice," Isabel quickly added. "Jaime had his tongue cut."

"That was certainly dramatic," observed Selma. "And so was yours, Isabel. By contrast my first experience is memorable because it was so unmemorable. What would you expect from a boy named Aaron Fink? Not Finkelstein, mind you—just plain Fink. But he was a very handsome ninth grader, who looked like a doctor even at the age of fifteen. But he was kinda dumb, especially about sex. Not only dumb, but finicky. When we kissed for the first time, he kept his mouth shut tight while I slobbered all over his lips trying to get him to French kiss me. No way! Not with Aaron. He resisted me all the way. Then he finally pulled apart and said, 'Look, Selma—I don't go for this dirty stuff. There are such things as germs, you know.' That's exactly what he said."

"You're kidding," said Jan. "You're making this up."

"Who would kid about a thing like that?"

"But what happened to him? I mean Aaron."

"You'll think I'm joking—but it's the God's honest truth: Aaron's a microbiologist for the Atomic Energy Commission. Undoubtedly the dumbest microbiologist in the whole country."

Now it was Jan's turn to tell about her initiation to

sex at the age of puberty, and her manner was tentative and obviously reluctant.

"My first experience was sort of comical at the beginning, but then it got pretty messy. I was about eleven at the time, and so was my cousin Joey. Anyway, we were playing hide-and-seek one night with some of the neighborhood kids; so Joey and I were hiding in a woodshed behind the house next door, huddling close together in this narrow space between a stack of logs and an outdoor freezer. Then suddenly he started kissing my right cheek and pressing himself against me, finally pushing his knee between my legs and hugging me so tight it sort of scared me. But I just laughed and pulled away from him, knocking some logs off the stack and making such a noise that somebody found our hiding place and easily tagged us.

"Well, the very next day, which was Saturday, my cousin Joey went to confession at St. Dominic's Church and told the priest that he had raped me!"

"You're kidding."

"No, I'm not. That's exactly what he did. You see, he was awfully religious. In fact, he was already an altar boy for the early-morning mass. So he had this guilt habit of confessing even his bad thoughts. And of course he didn't know what rape really was. . . ."

"But he felt guilty anyway," whispered Ruth.

"That's right. His darned guilt caused him to overconfess."

"So then what happened?"

"Well, a couple of days later this worried young priest went to Joey's house and told his parents about the confession, and they promptly came over to see my mom and dad. Then Joey and I were called into this two-family conference and had to explain what really happened. . . ."

"How did they keep from laughing?"

"They didn't. At least not my father and Uncle Tony. They almost choked with laughter."

"But how could he do that?" Ruth interrupted. "I mean the priest. They're not supposed to reveal what's told in confession."

"Some of them do," said Jan. "I guess there are blabbermouths in any profession. Rules or no rules."

"Well, I certainly wouldn't tell them anything. You can bet on that!"

"How about telling *us*, Ruth?" suggested Trudy. "It's your turn."

There was a long interval of silence, longer than usual. Then Ruth's hesitant voice.

"I don't think I can. At least not tonight. It had to do with my darned mother's reaction to what happened. She could be an awful bitch at times. . . ."

"My God—she said it!" exclaimed Graciela. "These sessions are really affecting us."

"What are you talking about?"

"Ruth just said 'bitch.' And she's never used that kind of word. You're loosening up, Ruthie. That's great!"

"Maybe. But I still can't use those other two words that come so easily to the rest of you."

"You mean 'shit' and 'fuck'?"

"Yes, those are the words. I still think it would be nicer to say something like 'excrement' or 'intercourse.' They're equally accurate, you know."

"But not as literary," said Graciela. "You'd never read such roundabout words in something by Mailer. It's always 'fuck' and 'shit' when he writes."

"Not always," Selma was quick to remind her. "I still remember one of the early Jack Paar shows, when Tallulah Bankhead was introduced to Mailer. She said, 'Oh, yes—you're the young man who can't spell *fuck*.' And Mailer just—"

"But how *did* he spell it?" asked Ruth.

129

"He'd write *frig* instead of fuck and *friggin'* instead of fuckin'. Or he'd write s--- or f---, just like all other writers. . . . And, by the way, dear sisters, it's time to close this friggin' meeting."

"Okay, Selma," said Jan with a rush. "But I've got one more question that I've been meaning to ask: Is your husband as funny as you are?"

"Wellll. . . . Our humor is sorta different. He's pornographic, while I'm merely graphic."

VII

Needless Surgery—
Hopeless Analysis

It is at her first abortion that woman begins to "know." For many women the world will never be the same.

—SIMONE DE BEAUVOIR

ONLY six of the women were present when the meeting began at five minutes past eight, and Selma immediately explained Graciela's absence.

"She may or may not come tonight. She called around noon and told me she was taking her niece to an abortionist."

"My God!" exclaimed Ruth with a catch in her throat. "I hope it's a legal one."

"It can't be," said Selma. "Her damned parents would have to consent, and the poor girl was afraid to tell them. They're Catholics and reactionary as hell. So she finally went to Aunt Graciela for help."

"Where did they go?"

"Out of town somewhere. To a motel. It's one of those sleazy hit-and-run deals by a doctor who wouldn't give his real name." Sad and weary bitterness in Selma's voice. "Graciela was worried as hell. She wanted to take

Olivia down to Mexico City—to a first-class clinic—but the girl's boyfriend has already made the arrangements."

"Well, at least *he* sounds responsible."

"Not much, Trudy. . . . He said he'd pay for the damned abortion, but he was going to let her go alone."

"The dirty bastard!" snapped Rachel. "What kind of a louse would—"

"He's a married schoolteacher about ten or fifteen years older than she is. They met at the bookstore where Olivia works weekends."

"Has Graciela met him?"

"Nope—he refused to see her. They talked only by phone, with her niece initiating the call for him—like some crappy TV soap opera."

"How long has she been pregnant?"

"That's another problem," Selma answered. "She's in her tenth or eleventh week, which is a fairly dangerous period for a D and C."

"What's a D and C?" asked Ruth.

"Dilatation and curettage—otherwise known as a scraping job. That's when the cervix is dilated with certain instruments so as to permit the doctor to insert a surgical knife called a curette, which scrapes the fetus off the uterine wall."

"You sound pretty knowledgeable," observed Isabel admiringly.

"Why not? I've had three scrapings in my short but lurid life."

"But that sounds awfully dangerous," said Ruth. "Especially in a motel."

"It certainly is," agreed Selma. "But we'd better get on with our scheduled topic for tonight—money problems in marriage. We'll talk more about abortions when we have our meeting on female medical problems."

"Why wait?" asked Rachel. "Now that we're into

132

this thing, we should go ahead. There's no law against switching topics."

"She's right," two or three voices chorused more or less together. "Let's switch."

"Okay with me," said Selma. "But I wanted to wait for Graciela to be here for that discussion."

"You won't have to wait," said someone, apparently turning away from the hidden microphone nearest her. "I think that's her car pulling into the driveway. . . ."

There was a babble of greetings and hurried inquiries as Graciela joined the group a minute later, her somewhat-breathless voice finally coming into clear focus:

". . . Olivia's fine. She'll be okay. But it was awful, just awful. That was undoubtedly the dreariest motel I've ever seen. Mucky gray walls, messy sink, spooky lighting, and the damned sheets hadn't been changed since God knows when. They actually smelled like ten stale orgasms. I mean really! So I went to the goddamned manager and got a couple of clean ones, and that stupid little butcher—with alcohol on his breath and these blubbery wet lips—kept telling me to cool it, not to bother anyone. . . . I would have called it off right there and then, but Olivia didn't want to wait any longer. She was getting a little panicky. But I insisted on clean sheets. And then I started praying like hell, every stupid Catholic prayer I've been trying to forget for the last ten years. Then one-two-three, it was over before you knew it. In less than five minutes. . . ."

"You're kidding!"

"No, I'm not, Trudy. That's all it took. He used this new suction technique. What they call a uterine aspirator. His nurse told me the name. Now *she* was okay. Clean, efficient, and sympathetic—as if she really cared. But all that doctor could think about was his goddamned

133

fee, though I'll have to admit he seemed pretty competent when he got started."

"What did he charge?"

"Five hundred and twelve dollars. The twelve dollars was for the lousy room. We weren't supposed to have any contact with the manager. But since I did, I gave him a five-dollar tip for the sheets."

"Where's Olivia now?"

"At my house. I didn't let her go back to the college dorm. And I hired that nurse to stay with her till tomorrow. I left your phone number with her, Selma— just in case."

"How about your husband, Raul? Does he know what's going on?"

"Well, fortunately, he's at the company office in Mexico this week, so I don't have to worry about him."

"Would he mind?"

"Oh, definitely. He's a hundred percent Catholic on the abortion issue. He'd probably insist on telling my sister and brother-in-law. I'm sure of that. Raul has always—"

"Excuse me, Graciela," said a timid voice. "I'm sorry to interrupt this way. But could you explain how this suction technique works?"

"Sure, Ruth. It's really quite simple. And apparently less dangerous than a D and C. They use a tubular instrument with a hole near the tip, and it's attached to a larger tube that's really a vacuum pump—like a miniature Hoover. There's also a receptacle that receives the fetus when it's loosened and sucked out of the uterus. So you avoid the danger of puncturing the uterine wall with the surgical knife that's generally used in a D and C."

"What if the fetus won't come loose?"

"Well, I asked the nurse about that on our way to my house, and she told me this uterine aspirator seldom

134

fails. But if it should, the doctor's got to be prepared to scrape with a knife."

"It's still awful," Ruth insisted. "Even with the simpler method. Especially when you consider the danger of infection in some sleazy motel."

"And think of all the women and teen-age girls who have to face that shit all by themselves—like that damned teacher expected Olivia to do." Resigned bitterness in Graciela's voice. "Thousands and thousands of women risking death or sterility because the goddamned Catholic Church won't allow safe legal abortions. I wouldn't rejoin that lousy church if my life depended on it."

"It's not only the Catholics who oppose abortions," said Jan defensively. "There are also quite a few Protestants."

"Yes, I know all about Nixon and his letter to Cardinal Cooke, which is the most obvious grab for the Catholic vote I've ever heard of. But it's still the damned church that's leading the fight against any kind of birth control. All over the world, Jan. And why should a bunch of pious celibate eunuchs have control over what women do with their own bodies?"

"Them's harsh words," said Rachel, though she obviously agreed.

"I've been feeling a lot harsher. *Bitter* would be more accurate. Thinking about my poor niece all last night and this morning and watching that scared helpless look in her face, I got into the bitterest rage you can possibly imagine. I kept remembering Father Ortiz, this scrawny, dry-lipped priest, preaching against contraception and warning his female parishioners that abortion was the next thing to murder and certainly a mortal sin. Scaring hell out of all those poor silly women who swallowed that garbage—including me."

"You?"

"That's right, Rachel."

"I can't believe you'd ever accept such nonsense."

"I certainly did—until I got to college. You can't imagine how guilt-ridden I was, even when I got into those hot necking sessions with Jaime."

"Well, you're not alone in the guilt department," said Trudy, breaking a momentary silence. "I was loaded with guilt for at least a month after my first abortion. I've had two. But the first one was the worst. I went down to Juárez, Mexico with a girlfriend and paid for all of it out of my own savings. The damned bastard who got me pregnant copped out immediately. 'How do I know it's mine?' he asked with this silly-ass smile, as if I were laying every man in town. 'But I'll give you a hundred anyway,' he said. And that's when I let him have it. . . ."

"What did you do?"

"Well, let me set the scene for you. First of all, we were sitting in this pancake house near his law office; and he was wearing a brand-new expensive summer suit that he'd bragged about as we sat down. And having a pig's appetite, he had ordered Swedish pancakes with huge gobs of soft butter and gooey blueberry syrup. So as he started to hand me that lousy hundred-dollar bill, I reached over and dumped that piled-up plate onto his lap, smearing his coat and pants with the worse mess I've ever seen—"

Roars of approving laughter and applause temporarily drowned out her giggling voice.

"Then I calmly got up and walked out of that restaurant like a model wearing a Christian Dior. I was bursting with pride."

"You should have been!" someone yelled.

"But then," continued Trudy in a suddenly-weary tone. "Then came the terrible part. That visit to Juárez.

We stayed in a very nice motel, but the doctor's office scared me stiff."

"Did he speak English?"

"Oh, yes. Fairly good English, with all the appropriate slang. Most of his clients are American. But his office was filthy and smelly and poorly lit, with crooked venetian blinds that hadn't been cleaned in years. And his bitten-off fingernails seemed to be clotted with dried blood as if they'd scraped a thousand uteruses or whatever the plural is. But, apparently noticing how I'd stared at them, he self-consciously announced that he always washed his hands and rubber gloves in hot water before every operation—six or seven times every weekend night, Friday, Saturday, and Sunday."

"My God, Trudy. He must make a mint."

"He sure does. But he's got to divide it several ways—police, judges, and hundreds of American doctors who send him clients. I'll bet my doctor got at least a third of the six hundred I had to pay. They sounded awfully chummy when my doctor called Juárez to arrange my appointment."

"Did you have any complications?" asked Isabel.

"Plenty. And that was the scariest part. I started bleeding when Doris got me back to the motel—bleeding and cramping. So Doris rushed back to his office (he didn't have a listed phone) and tried to get him to come right away. But he told her I'd have to wait a few hours. He had another appointment across the border in El Paso, with, he proudly explained, 'a very rich Americana who insists that I go to her fancy motel.' So I had to wait until way past midnight, trying not to cry as Doris kept changing and washing out the towels, ringing them as dry as she could by looping them around the shower pipe. But she was soon able to get a dozen clean towels from a wonderfully kind chambermaid who refused to take a tip, probably aware of what they were needed for.

. . . Well, fortunately, the bleeding had almost stopped by the time Dr. Velez arrived, and he gave me a douche that sterilized the wound. Then he cautioned me not to take any sleeping pills—that I'd soon fall asleep without them . . ."

"Did you?"

"Strangely enough, I did. Doris gave me a warm glass of milk that put me to sleep for twelve solid hours. . . . Now tell us about those three abortions you had, Selma."

"Well, I guess my luck was better than yours, especially with the men who knocked me up. The first abortion was performed by my boyfriend's uncle in his very hygienic private clinic, and Hal was with me from beginning to end. Couldn't have been sweeter. We spent the night at his family's fancy beach house, attended by the uncle's most experienced nurse. And Hal brought me a dozen white roses and a bottle of ginger ale."

"Why ginger ale?"

"Because that's what I had used for the douche that didn't work. So that became our private joke. He sent me a whole crate of twenty-four bottles for my birthday."

"But why did you use ginger ale?"

"Some dumb sorority sister said it would always work in an emergency. 'Just shake it well so it fizzes a lot,' she told us. 'Then push the neck of the bottle inside you and let the fizzy ale wash you out.' But—as you can easily guess—most of it whooshed out before I could get it inside me."

"Now that," said Rachel, still chuckling with the others, "is about the most original soft-drink commercial I've ever heard!"

"What about the other two abortions?" asked Trudy.

"Same good luck. Both of them resulted from some delightful but much-too-spontaneous sex with the man who later married me. And I've got to admit, he was fantastically gentle and helpful. Worried more than my mother would have worried. Made all of the arrangements for a very clean D and C and never left my side from beginning to end. So how could I *not* marry a man like that—when I finally forced him to beg me?"

"Any other abortions for this group?"

"I had one a few years ago," said Rachel. "About two years after I got married to Jerry. As a matter of fact, Jerry's cousin did the scraping at his own office, and I went back to rehearsals that same afternoon."

"Rehearsals for what?"

"For that TV soap opera I used to do. But the only point I'm making is that it was clean and simple, the way all abortions *could* be if we didn't have such stupid laws. Only women with money or connections can really be safe, which excludes most black people. And also Puerto Ricans and Chicanos."

"And poor whites," someone added.

"My single abortion was a damned nightmare," said Graciela. "But with all that's happened today, I'd rather not talk about it right now."

"I don't blame you," said Ruth. "Neither would I. But before we get off the subject, I'd still like to know why there's been so much opposition to legalizing abortions."

"Because legalized abortions would be another step—a most important step—to real freedom for women. And that would be too much of a threat for the so-called Establishment."

"So you think it's basically political?"

"It certainly is, Ruthie. And it's politics at the most fundamental level." This was Selma talking in a rare (for her) moment of total seriousness, with no hint of her characteristic levity. "And if I'm not making myself clear enough, let me read you this passage from an essay on

139

birth control by a sister named Lucinda Cisler. She's really fantastic. Here she is:

> . . . Since her basic function has been to bear children, whatever "extra" activities the culture and the economy have allowed her to pursue, *anything that alters social control over her reproductive capacities is deeply and fundamentally threatening to societal and individual psyches:* different reproductive roles are THE basic dichotomy in humankind, and have been used to rationalize all the other, ascribed differences between men and women and to justify all the oppression women have suffered.
>
> Without the full capacity to limit her own reproduction, a woman's other "freedoms" are tantalizing mockeries that cannot be exercised. With it, the others cannot long be denied, since the chief rationale for denial disappears.
>
> This is one very practical reason why the older movements for women's liberation could not go beyond hollow token gains; medical technology had not yet developed effective contraception and safe abortion techniques (nor had male law and custom placed a high priority on such developments). Women wanting to be something besides reproducers had to choose sexual abstinence, masturbation, or homosexuality, trust to luck and crude birth-control methods, or rely on hired substitutes to take care of the resulting children. (Italics supplied.)

Graciela was the first one to comment on what Selma had read: "It's the very last line—that phrase about *care of the resulting children*—which raises another set of problems. Once you have them, *who's* going to raise them? That's the real rub."

"How about day care centers?"

"There aren't many good ones, Isabel. Even so, you can't send your kids till they're three or four. So you've still got those first three miserable years that will tie you

140

down . . . twelve hours a day if you're conscientious."

"There are some day care centers that take them pretty early, Graciela."

"Not my kids."

"I thought you had teen-agers."

"I do, but I was just thinking back to an earlier time, and how I probably screwed up my own two kids by leaving them with a middle-aged neighbor. While I went off to teach school. And that's a load of guilt that's still weighing me down."

"How so?"

"Because I was copping out. That old woman was a martinet, and I damned well knew it! She wouldn't let Jose and Erlinda do anything that might dirty the house or mess up their room. No fooling with finger paints or clay, no hollering or playing wild or anything else that would release their natural energy or exercise their curiosity. Behave, behave, behave—that's all she understood."

"So why did you keep her?"

"Because the house was always spotlessly clean when I got home, and there was always a nice homemade casserole dish in the oven. And the kids were always quiet and well behaved. Perhaps I should say 'traumatized into silence.' But I didn't see it that way until I started reading some of the earlier Montessori stuff. That's when I fired her, quit teaching, and promptly went to the other extreme, creating my own version of a Summerhill bedlam."

"That bad?"

"Well . . . I guess I'm exaggerating, Ruth. But I was trying so hard to undo what Mrs. Jensen had done to them, to sort of loosen them up, that I must have confused them worse than ever. So now I've got a screwed-up little bitch on my hands—I mean Erlinda—and it's mostly my fault."

"Now you're accepting the old mother myth—hook, line, and sinker," protested Rachel. "You haven't even mentioned your husband's role in all this."

"Perhaps you're right, Rachel. He's got his share of blame. But when I read this recent stuff by Jerome Bruner on early childhood development, I'm inclined to believe that mothers really do have the greater burden and responsibility. There is something symbiotic between mother and child. We can't escape it."

"Now you're getting highbrow," said Jan teasingly. "What does that fancy word mean?"

"It means—or I *think* it means—some kind of organic connection. Like the kind a woman necessarily has with her unborn child. And I think that prenatal connection has to carry over in a psychological and emotional sense, a certain dependency that goes both ways."

"Yes, but that dependency isn't as great (or demanding) as we've been led to believe," observed Selma. "That's part of the motherhood mystique which a *macho* society keeps foisting on us. Babies could be a lot more independent than they are. They could conceivably be better off without either parent feeding them their own neuroses. And, incidentally, there's no reason why fathers can't raise them just as effectively as mommies. There's no—"

"Oh, Selma, that's a silly pipe dream," Ruth interrupted with uncustomary emphasis. "We couldn't expect men to suddenly give up their jobs, leave their law offices and clinics or garages, to stay home with their babies. That would never happen!"

"Why not? there have been matriarchal societies, you know. Since way back in history."

"Well, it won't happen in this country. At least not in our lifetime. So I think it's silly and a hopeless waste of time to even think about it, much less talk about it."

142

"Maybe you're right," said Selma. "Of course you are. And, besides, I personally wouldn't want to live in a matriarchy. I'd rather *kvetch* at the men for having wars and garbage strikes than to have them *kvetching* at us. As a matter of fact, I'm convinced that those smart Jews in Israel have deliberately laid the groundwork for an eventual matriarchy by electing a nice Yiddish grandmother to be President. And when you get a bunch of women running that country, the damned Arabs will finally conclude that Israel isn't worth retaking. Because why would the Jewish men give it up? . . . So while you're thinking about my priceless solution for the Near East crisis, we'll have some tea and coffee."

Ten minutes later the formal discussion was resumed with Rachel calling their attention to another passage from Robin Morgan's anthology of writings from the Women's Liberation Movement, *Sisterhood Is Powerful*: "I've been skimming through Selma's copy, and I'd like to read a paragraph she underlined on page two hundred and fifty-four:

> But the study of family power relations and contraceptive practices cannot tell us everything we need to know. There is a profound fear of woman's sexual potential behind the continuing insistence that (for women) sexuality and reproduction are inseparable, the physical fact is that in women these functions are potentially *more* distinct than they are in men: as Masters and Johnson pointed out quite explicitly—in a passage that seems to have been printed in invisible ink, judging from the attention paid it—the clitoris is unique in that it is the only organ in human anatomy whose purpose is exclusively that of erotic excitation and release. It is the multi-functional penis—carrier of both semen and of sexual nervous response (among other things)—that in every sexual act is simultaneously procreative and erotic. Can men's unconscious

143

realization of these truths, as well as the understand-able desire to believe what is most convenient for their own needs in intercourse, underlie the stubborn ortho-dox-Freudian insistence that the seat of "mature" female sexuality must be the vagina. *When an oppressed group has a profound natural advantage like this one (a special erotic organ), the dominant group cannot rest until it has convinced most of the subordinate ones that they are in fact disadvantaged in this way as in all others. . . .*

"That's so true," exclaimed Isabel. "That's why the Arabs have always mutilated their women by cutting off their clitoris. They can't stand the sexual threat."

"That's dreadful," said Ruth. "I can't imagine anything so painful. Where did you hear about that?"

"Read it somewhere. A long time ago. And I've heard there are plenty of clitorectomies performed in the country. For psychological reasons, they say."

"The same shitty reasons they always give when they're mutilating women with surgery." Sudden acute anger in Rachel's usually easygoing manner. "My aunt had a hysterectomy for *quote* psychological reasons *unquote*, and she never recovered from that damned operation! 'I'm no longer a woman,' she kept telling me. 'They've taken away my nature, honey, they cut it out of me.' I can still remember her exact words, because she repeated them so often. And then she'd say, 'Don't let anyone cut out your uterus, child—no matter what jive they lay on you.' Crying herself to sleep every night. . . ."

"How old were you when this happened?"

"About fifteen or sixteen, Jan. That terrible vulnera-ble age, when I'd become so acutely aware of my own female organs. I'd have these awful nightmares, where this stranger with a white mask would be chasing me through a maze of empty corridors trying to cut out my insides, and I'd wake up screaming my aunt's name—

Corrie, Corrie, Corrie. But I'd never tell anyone what I was dreaming. For some strange reason, I was afraid that if I told anyone, that if I should put that nightmare into actual words, then it would really happen."

"But what were the so-called *psychological reasons* for performing that hysterectomy on your Aunt Corrie?"

"It was supposed to relieve her anxieties during menopause, and it merely multiplied them."

"So, like most female surgery, the cure is worse than the ill," said Selma. "And somewhere I've read (or heard) that eighty percent of all hysterectomies are unnecessary surgery."

"That's true about a lot of surgery," added Jan. "For men as well as women."

"Yes, but it's mostly women who run into knife-happy surgeons, particularly gynecologists."

"You're exaggerating!" protested Ruth. "You're condemning a whole profession, including my husband. I can't believe that Walter operates on women unnecessarily. I really couldn't live with that, Trudy."

"Well, I'm not so sure about *my* husband," said Isabel. "I've always been disturbed by offhand wisecracks I've heard from him and his fellow doctors at cocktail parties or at their medical conventions. Little jokes about 'vaginal surpluses' and seven-hundred-dollar bladders. The money angle is always part of the picture. . . ."

"But they're *joking,* Isabel. I've heard Walter making the same wisecracks; but I've always considered it like—well, like shop talk or something like that."

"Humor," said Trudy, "especially that kind of sick humor, is sometimes a pretty good mask for what people really think. It's like all those women-hating nightclub comedians who only *pretend* they're kidding when they insult their wives and mothers-in-law. So doctors joke about unnecessary operations because they actually perform them."

145

"That almost happened to Shari about a year ago," Selma recalled with an edge of resentment. "We were vacationing near Denver, when she started cramping and suddenly passed out. And the first doctor who examined her immediately recommended surgery and got angry with me when I hesitated. Alvin, by the way, wasn't there. He was to join us a few days later. But, anyway, this doctor was annoyed with me and even hinted that I was risking Shari's life. Nevertheless, I called this pediatrician in Denver, a friend of Alvin's, and he told me to hold off until *he* got there. So two hours later, he examined her, made a couple of tests, and told me no surgery was necessary. She'd merely had a sudden metabolic assault owing to an unusually prolonged menstrual period. That was all—nothing really serious. But that first knife-happy bastard was all ready to cut her open."

"You should have reported him to the medical association."

"I did. I wrote them a long letter and even asked the second doctor to write a collaborating letter. But he wouldn't do it. He gave me some half-ass reason about 'excusable mistakes' that aren't necessarily negligent."

"And what about the medical association?"

"Are you kidding, Jan?" Selma sneered. "All I got from them was a form letter thanking me for my concern and assuring me that 'proper inquiries' will be made. And never heard from them again."

"Just the same," said Graciela. "We should always write letters to the medical associations when things like that happen—and send Xerox copies to the doctor. It may not stop them altogether from performing unnecessary surgery, but they might possibly—just possibly—perform a few less than before."

"Don't count on it, sweetie."

146

"But how can we ever know when surgery *is* or *isn't* necessary?" asked Jan.

"First of all, we can always ask for an opinion from another doctor, preferably someone connected with a different hospital. But, in the final analysis, we've got to have more female doctors."

"But why, Trudy? How can we be sure they won't be just as callous and money-minded?"

"We can't. But I'll bet a female doctor will have a far better understanding about the psychological effects of most female operations, especially about such things as hysterectomies. They'd have to be more sensitive."

"You're right," said Isabel. "You're right as you can be. I've had a female gynecologist for several years. So has my daughter, Linda. And, believe me, I've never had such expert treatment. What's more, she's patient and gentle, although just as efficient as any man. And she never gives us that patronizing don't-worry-about-it crap I used to get from my former doctor."

"I know *that* scene," Rachel agreed. "All I got from my gynecologist were insults and finger fucking. That's all it—"

"This is making me sick," said Ruth in an anguished half whisper. "My head's spinning. I keep thinking about my husband, and it's making me sick. . . ."

"I'm sorry. I wasn't implying—"

"No, it's nothing *you* said, Rachel. It's this whole conversation. But I'm not blaming anyone. You've got to say these things because you really believe them—because you've actually experienced them. I know you have. And that's the terrible part. Because I'm beginning to feel that other women may be saying the same things about my husband. And I know that he's impatient and sarcastic with some of his female patients, because he's

147

often sarcastic with me—not just as a person, but as a female. He really doesn't like women, and certainly doesn't respect them. . . ."

There was a long pause before she continued, and there was a dead silence from everyone else in the room.

"So that I can easily believe—no, not too easily—it's really hard to believe—but I guess I'm beginning to believe that Walter could now and then perform an unnecessary hysterectomy on someone. Though I doubt that he could ever admit it—even to himself. He's not likely to admit anything about himself. As a matter of fact, I've never heard him admit he was wrong about anything. Nor apologize to anyone."

"That's awfully sad," observed Isabel. "He must be terribly insecure."

"I guess he is," said Ruth. "Although he doesn't seem to be. Outwardly, I mean. He's always tough and self-assertive."

"Are most surgeons that way?"

"They've got to be, Trudy. Would you want a surgeon who acts unsure of himself?"

"No, I guess not."

"Well, how about a psychoanalyst?" asked Jan. "Should he be the same way?"

It was Rachel who supplied the ready answer. "Honey, he *can't* be as sure of himself as a surgeon. If he were that sure of himself, he wouldn't be an analyst. It's his insecurities that drew him into that profession in the first place. And that's why he's so good at spotting someone else's insecurities."

"Bravo!" yelled Selma. "You've been describing my husband to the nth degree."

"Now that you've mentioned Alvin," said Isabel, "do you think he ever performs unnecessary therapy?"

"In what respect?"

148

"Does he have patients who really don't need him?"

"Gee, Isabel, I've never thought about that possibility. Though I guess he might. Psychoanalysis is such a tricky relationship. All kinds of dependencies develop—both ways. But I guess there could be some unnecessary therapy."

"It's more than *could be*, sweetie," said Rachel emphatically. "There *is* a lot of unnecessary therapy. And some of that *dependency* you mentioned is mostly a financial dependency. Some patients, especially the rich ones, become economic crutches for the analyst. I know a woman, for example, who has been going to the same damned shrink for twenty years. Five times a week at thirty bucks a visit, and that's what I call a guilt-edged annuity."

"You're kidding," said Jan. "You must be kidding. Why would it take so long to cure someone?"

"That's never been his intention, Jan. Quite obviously, that poor gal is just one of his better meal tickets and a damned expensive one."

"But what does her husband say about it?"

"Can't say a damned thing. It's her money. She's loaded with it. And that doctor knows it, knew it from the very beginning."

"There are plenty of cases like that," observed Trudy. "Though not quite as extreme. In fact, I recently read something (I think it was a novel) about this analyst who cultivated a bunch of rich neurotic women who paid him for what he called sexual therapy. He was like a fifty-dollar-a-lay call girl, except that he enjoyed professional respectability."

Bursting into laughter, Rachel finally controlled herself enough to say, "He must have been one of those lay analysts I've heard about."

"There're plenty of those," said Selma. "One of my

149

husband's colleagues has frequently gotten into hot water because of this sex bit. He can't resist crawling onto the couch with his female patients."

"Nevertheless, you've gone way way overboard in your griping about analysts," said Graciela quite emphatically. "I had a couple of years of analysis, and it was the best thing that ever happened to me. In fact, I couldn't have stayed with this group, listening to all this heavy stuff we've been unloading, if I hadn't gone through those painful but eventually helpful sessions with Dr. Steiner—Rosalind Steiner—about the most fantastic person I've ever known."

"A female analyst?"

"That's right, Ruth. And I'd recommend her to anyone. Man or woman. When I first went to see her, I was nearly suicidal. The most defeated, self-pitying person you could possibly imagine. I saw the whole world lined up against me. Ready to tear me apart. The slightest disagreement with anyone—about the most trivial matter—would become an indirect threat that would suddenly balloon into an outright attack. My dearest friends were suddenly conniving enemies. And my husband was obviously the chief conspirator, who had married me just to get on the inside. . . . But somehow, through the subtlest kind of magic and deep, deep compassion, Dr. Steiner gradually pulled me out of that god-awful mess and gave me the courage to face my own failings. So, you see, I really can't tolerate people attacking all analysts."

"But we're going overboard in our criticism of all doctors," warned Jan. "Which worries me a little. In fact, it worries me a lot. That's why I'm so skeptical about this new Feminist Woman's Health Center in Los Angeles."

"What's wrong with it?"

"Well, to be frank with you, I'm leary as hell about

150

all that self-help gynecology they're pushing. How would a bunch of nonprofessional women know all about our female disorders?"

"They don't claim to know everything," said Trudy. "You've been reading all that negative shit in the papers, most of it generated by the AMA and antifeminist doctors."

"Then what are they doing?"

"They're simply showing women how to diagnose some of their own physical ailments, the simpler, more common ones. I went to a lecture by Carol Downer and Lorraine Rothman when they were on a cross-country tour for the center, and they used slides and film to show us how to examine our own bodies. And to tell you the God's honest truth that's the first time I'd ever seen a vagina and clitoris in living color. . . ."

Bursts of laughter and giggling comments temporarily smothered Trudy's voice, but quickly faded as she continued.

"They showed us simple infections on the vaginal or clitoral surface that we can cure ourselves with ordinary first-aid medication, without having to rush to a gynecologist for expensive lab tests and long-faced speculations that cost fifteen dollars for a lousy five minutes. . . . Look, Jan, it's just the same as some man cutting the tender skin on his penis with a cunt hair or just irritating it with what my doctor once called coital friction. No man would rush off to a doctor for a simple thing like that: He'd merely treat it with a dab of disinfectant cream . . . and maybe bitch a little because he can't screw for a couple of days. . . . But, getting back to my point about the center's self-help gynecology, it could save us all from a lot of useless treatment and unnecessary surgery. So I'm perfectly willing to put up with an exaggeration here and there."

"Maybe you're right," said Jan. "I hadn't looked at it that way. I've just been worried about the criticisms from the medical associations."

"Well, as far as I'm concerned, they'd be in a much better position to criticize if they'd occasionally blast a few of their own members for some of the crap they dish out."

"And on that high note, we'll have to close," said Selma. "But first of all, I'd like to tell you about some unnecessary surgery on a male. It happened to my cousin Loren. He got a vasectomy five years ago because he didn't want any more kids. Then he found out his wife couldn't conceive anyway. So he got himself untied because the vasectomy had made him feel less *macho*. But it hasn't worked. His sperm count is still only ten percent—even though he eats two dozen oysters every night."

"He should sue for malpractice," said Rachel.

"He has," said Selma.

There was a long pause and a shuffling of chairs as someone started to serve a second round of coffee and sandwiches, and finally Selma called their attention to a conversation she had just had with Ruth. "Before we get off the subject of malpractice, Ruth has something to tell us."

"It's about my husband, Walter, and one of his female patients," said Ruth after clearing her throat. "For a couple of months last year, this woman kept calling him at home, sometimes way after midnight. And when she'd start screaming, he'd hold the phone away from his ear, and I could hear her yelling, 'You're a butcher—you're a butcher—you're a goddamned butcher!' Then she'd suddenly hang up with huge sobs in her throat. . . ."

"And what would he say?"

"Nothing. Nothing at all. He'd roll out of bed,

disconnect the phone from the wall socket, and go back
to sleep without saying a word."

"He probably thought you were asleep."

"Well, he *pretended* I was. And so did I."

"And you never asked him about the calls?"

"Yes—I finally did. I asked him about them the
morning after the third or fourth call, and he simply
shrugged it off with his usual cool indifference. 'Just some
crazy dame,' he said. 'Complaining about a hysterectomy. She asked for it, and now she's bitching about it.'
So then I asked him if she needed the operation, and he
told me to quit bugging him. . . . Anyway, a few days
later, when Walter was out of town, she called again, and
I answered the phone. Then, apparently sensing that I'd
be willing to listen to her, she gave me her version of the
story. . . .'"

"What did she say?"

"Well, she cried quite a bit, but finally managed to
tell me that Walter and her husband had persuaded her
to have a hysterectomy—that they'd really pressured
her."

"But why?"

"Because her husband didn't want any more children, although they only had one. And Walter had
convinced her that it was a simple operation with no bad
aftereffects."

"How old was she?"

"Only thirty-three. And she'd been perfectly
healthy, she told me. Active in all kinds of community
affairs. And now she's a nervous wreck."

"But why—if her damned husband was so anxious
about not having any more kids—why didn't Walter
advise *him* to have a vasectomy?"

"That's what I finally asked him," said Ruth. "But I
didn't ask him that question (or any other questions)
until last Thursday night, when we had our big argu-

ment. The minute I got home from our meeting, I walked into the bedroom and said, 'Walter, I'd like to talk with you about Barbara Finley, the woman who kept calling you last year about that hysterectomy.' And when he tried to put me off, telling me it was all in the past, a dead issue, I wouldn't let him off the hook. I kept badgering him with questions, which finally became accusations. 'Your only concern was her damned husband's convenience,' I finally told him. 'You didn't give a damn about her—you couldn't care less about the psychological damage you might be causing!' And that's when he called me a goddamned stupid peacenik bitch! As if it were one continuous word. And I came back at him with something I'd never done before. . . ."

"What was that?"

"I called him a dirty bastard," said Ruth with obvious satisfaction. "I wanted to call him a *shitty* bastard, but I couldn't bring myself to say that word. Although I was certainly thinking it. . . ."

Pausing to accept their approving cheers and applause, she went on in a more pensive mood.

"So we've been arguing back and forth ever since, and my determination to leave him has been increasing every day. But I've had moments of great doubt and confusion. And fear, I guess. Fear of suddenly being alone. I know that he's cold and unloving, that he's much more of a sexist than I'd ever imagined; but he's always been there—as a kind of protector, if nothing else. Yet there's no point in—well, I mean there's no sense in staying with someone you can never love again. So I guess I'll go back to teaching fourth graders."

"When was the last time you taught, Ruth?"

"About fourteen years ago. So I'll need a few refresher courses."

"But you won't have to work, will you?"

"Not as far as the money's concerned, Jan. We're

pretty well off. But I'd like to feel useful, especially since I have no children."

"Would you keep the house?"

"I don't think so. I'd rather move into an apartment and get rid of all the damned responsibility of running a house."

"You'll get a good price for it, Ruth."

"But Walter will handle the sale. I've never gotten into that sort of thing, that's why everything's under his name—the house, the medical building, the bank accounts, the beach apartments, just about everything except my car."

"If that's the case," warned Rachel, breaking through several other voices expressing sudden concern, "you'd better get yourself a real sharp lawyer—preferably someone who doesn't belong to Walter's golf club."

"But why?"

"Because that sounds awfully suspicious, Ruthie. Putting all that property in his name only—that just doesn't sound kosher to me."

"That was only for business convenience, Rachel. His lawyer told me that. A long time ago."

"*His* lawyer, sweetie. Not yours."

"I'm beginning to see your point," said Ruth. "I've really been awfully innocent. But he's not going to get away with it. I'll fight him all the way."

"Right on!" said Isabel. "But you'd better let your lawyer do the fighting."

Someone, probably Jan, suggested that Trudy's husband might be asked to represent Ruth; but the suggestion was immediately vetoed by Trudy herself: "He's a pretty good divorce lawyer, but I'm afraid this would be an awkward time to ask him."

"How come?"

"Because I've also been contemplating a divorce, and John's convinced that these rap sessions have ruined

155

our marriage. He thinks we're all bitches or witches. And he knows Ruth is part of the group. So you can imagine how he'd react if she were to ask him to represent her in a divorce action. . . ."

"He'd probably throw me out," said Ruth.

"I'm afraid so," Trudy agreed. "He's in a bad bad mood these days."

"And what are *your* reasons for splitting up?" asked Graciela.

"The same reasons that have existed since Ronnie was two or three years old, when we discovered he was permanently handicapped with dyslexia and dyslalia. Almost immediately John started to ignore that child, refusing to play with him anymore and finally refusing to even look at him. He'd come home late every night, when Ronnie was sure to be asleep, and he wouldn't so much as peek into the boy's bedroom. And whenever I'd start to talk about Ronnie, he'd quickly change the subject or leave the room, pretending he'd left his damned pipe in another room."

"That's really weird, Trudy."

"It certainly is, Jan. And he's still ignoring Ronnie, perhaps more than ever."

"But where does he stay while he's waiting for his son to get out of sight—at the office or some neighborhood bar?"

"At some bar, I guess—with one of his young boyfriends," answered Trudy with a hint of resignation. "But his homosexuality hasn't bothered me half as much as his attitude toward Ronnie."

"But why has he wanted to stay married?"

"I frankly don't know, Rachel. Perhaps I'm a convenient cover for his extracurricular sex life. You know how stuffy the legal profession can be and the importance that's attached to marriage."

"So why haven't *you* cut out?"

156

"Because I've been stuck with a handicapped child and huge medical bills. If he were normal, I could have gone back to my job when he was old enough for a day care center. . . . But things have changed recently. I've located this wonderful school for brain-damaged kids. They're picked up in a station wagon at eight A.M. and they're returned at five P.M. So I'll be going back to work soon. My old associate has offered me a nice job in his new company, which produces educational films for science courses."

"That's wonderful," said Jan. "I certainly admire your courage. I couldn't do it—that's for sure."

"Why not?"

"Quite frankly, Selma, I'd be afraid to. I wouldn't be able to support myself."

"Of course you could, Jan!"

"No, I'm not kidding you. I'd really be lost. I've never had a job. I got married right out of high school, less than a week after graduation. So the only talent I've got is for housekeeping."

"You could easily be a sales clerk."

"Never. I'd be scared to death. I'd panic with all those customers crowding around me. So, no matter how bad my marriage gets, I'm stuck with it. At least until my kids grow up. But I guess most women are caught in the same trap. I'm not the only one, thank God. . . . And I'll tell you something else: I wouldn't know how to handle my money even if I could get a job. Ron has always taken care of everything at our house—paid all the bills, supervised any major purchases, and everything else that's financial. He's always been the moneyman. So what I need, I ask for—and if I play my cards right, I may get it. Or maybe only half of it. Depends on what mood he's in. But I'm not starving."

"Have you ever had a checking account?"

"Well, I suggested that once—about five years

157

ago—and Ron just laughed at me. 'With that brain of yours, the bank would go nuts trying to balance your checks,' he told me. And maybe he's right. I've always been bad with figures. That's why we finally gave up on the rhythm method. I couldn't keep track of when I'd menstruated the month before."

"That's why they call it Vatican Roulette," said Graciela. "Because it's always a wild gamble."

"It certainly is," agreed Jan. "And I lost at least twice. That's how we got Frank and Larry, my two youngest boys. The other three we planned for—I mean, it really didn't matter. Anyway, after Larry was born, we tried what Father Angelo called coitus interruptus, or pulling out before climax, which can be awfully messy when your husband comes as he's pulling out, and damned frustrating. Finally, Ron said I could use the pill—but never to confess that I did to Father Angelo."

Her statement was followed by a rather prolonged discussion of various contraception techniques, many of which had been mentioned at earlier meetings. One of the most bizarre methods of self-abortion was described by Graciela, who had read about it in a Mexican magazine. An impoverished Peruvian housewife, already burdened with too many half-starved children, had tried to dislodge a fetus from her uterus by scraping it with a crucifix. But contrary to most first impressions, she had not intended to be sacrilegious. She had, in fact, devoutly hoped that the unborn child would be blessed by the crucifix as it was aborted.

VIII

The Money Problem

"*The wife who married for money, compared with the prostitute*," says Havelock Ellis, "*is the true scab. She is paid less, gives much more in return in labor and care, and is absolutely bound to her master. The prostitute never signs away the right over her own person, she retains her freedom and personal rights, nor is she always compelled to submit to man's embrace.*"

—EMMA GOLDMAN,
Anarchism and Other Essays

"AFTER listening to some of the horror stories about medical malpractice in our meeting last week," said Selma, "I'm afraid most of our money problems will seem pretty trivial, but let's discuss them anyway. And I'd like to start with you, Jan, since you've already gotten into it. I'd like to know how you feel about your husband controlling all your finances."

"I simply accept it most of the time. Because I grew up in that kind of family—I mean where the head of the house makes all the money decisions. But sometimes—in fact, pretty damned often—Ron makes me feel like some kind of beggar. Like he'll ask me, 'What the hell did you do with the twenty bucks I gave you last Saturday?' As if I'm wasting his goddamned money on a lot of crap. So when I get mad enough, I'll tell him I've been flushing it down the goddamned john—or some other kooky thing. But most of the time I'll swallow my damned pride, and

159

I'll give him some sort of accounting—like four dollars for Mary's dance lesson, a dollar and a half for lunch when I'm shopping, seven dollars for new underwear, three dollars for his shirts at the Chinese laundry—and I can see his lips moving while he's adding it up in his head, making me feel sort of guilty like when I'm confessing to Father Angelo, and finally wanting to slap Ron's goddamned stupid face for making me feel that way, and wanting to cry because there's nothing else I can do. . . ."

Her voice had suddenly broken into sobs, and there were murmurs of comfort and pent-up angers, a swirl of remembered frustrations, someone mumbling, "We take so damn much shit," and someone else sadly commenting about "so many humiliations." Finally, when the criss-crossing voices had lapsed into a weary silence, Graciela started talking about the money problems at her house.

"I've got a kind of token freedom. Which means that I have my own checking account, but it's based on a monthly household allowance. So that my begging and cajoling takes place whenever I need a bigger allowance, and that's almost every month. Consequently, we have this thirty-day cycle of really bitter fights that might go on for three or four days. And that's when Raul's *machismo* goes into high gear. I'm now convinced that he gets an erection every time he scores a point against my new budget, and it's a total orgasm if he manages—"

Laughter drowning out her voice.

"—if he manages to hold me down to last month's allowance. Consequently, I've got to overwhelm him with cost-of-living figures from magazine articles, or maybe some lawyerlike exhibits one, two and three—like Er-linda's worn-out shoes, Jose's torn slacks, and a burned-out toaster. I'll put them all in a big suitcase beforehand, and then pull them out one by one as I present my case. . . ."

160

"You're kidding, Grace, you're putting us on."

"No, I'm not, Rachel. That's exactly what I do—almost every month."

"Sounds awfully funny."

"I know it does, but it's not very funny when you actually have to do it. In fact, it's pretty goddamned humiliating. As Jan was telling us before, they make you feel like a damned beggar. And Raul always puts on this superior manner, like the lord of the manor talking to a damned peasant. Sometimes, whenever I'm in the middle of one of those lousy money squabbles, I get the feeling that it would be more dignified to be a whore. And much simpler. She sets her price, and if the man doesn't want to pay it, he can take his hard-on somewhere else. . . ."

"Or get a free one at home," someone added.

"Not from me, he won't," said Selma with a suppressed chuckle. "I'm setting my own price from now on. Five dollars a trick . . . or maybe I'll pay him."

"That's it!" exclaimed Jan as Selma's voice abruptly faded to a mere whisper. "Now you're getting to the nitty-gritty. I know you're joking, Selma, but you're not really joking. You're really serious."

"About what?"

"About sex and wives and prostitutes."

"You've lost me, sweetie. I don't know where you're coming from. I really don't."

"Well, let's go back to the notion that wives are like whores—that they're actually selling themselves for a higher price. Which assumes that only men like sex, that women do it only for money. And that's pure nonsense. We like to screw just as much as they do, maybe more. As a matter of fact, if it was really necessary, I'd pay my husband to take me to bed. And that's what Selma was really talking about—even though she passed it off as a joke—when she said '*or I would pay him.*' "

"I guess you're right, Jan. I wasn't joking when I

161

said that," Selma admitted with a catch in her voice. "I get so little sex from Alvin nowadays that I'd really pay him—no, not him, but maybe some charity—pay him let's say, X number of dollars for every time he'd roll me in the hay."

"But why would you pay some charity rather than your husband?" asked Rachel, probably repressing a smile.

"Because it would damage his ego if I paid him directly."

"But more likely damage your ego."

"Probably so, Trudy. But it would—"

"Hey! This is getting wild," protested Graciela. "That's all nonsense. No woman's going to pay her husband a stud fee. Not in a million years. So let's get off this subject. It's not even worth joking about."

Murmurs of approval greeted her statement. Then Trudy's crisp voice sliced through the babble: "I think you're overreacting, Graciela. But let me get back to the point Jan was making about the difference between wives and whores. Now, if I understand you correctly—and I think I do—you're really telling us that wives get paid not for screwing but for housekeeping."

"That's right," said Jan. "And we're always under-paid. Our husbands couldn't afford us at union scales. For example, if I charged Ron just three dollars an hour, he'd have to pay me thirty-six dollars a day—which comes to . . . let's see now . . . seven times thirty-six is . . . two, carry four . . . times. . . ."

"It's two hundred and fifty-two dollars," said Trudy. "Or roughly one thousand dollars a month—without fringe benefits."

"Getting laid is the fringe benefit," said Jan. "And I'd settle for half that amount."

"So would I," Selma added. "But I'd demand a ten-hour day. Twelve hours is too much, sisters. And why not have a six-day week instead of the seven we're stuck with?"

"Well, there you have it," concluded Trudy, once again reverting to swift calculations. "We've got an eighty-four-hour week at substandard wages that are never paid. And not an ounce of bargaining. . . ."

This feeling of powerlessness, of economic impotence, was stressed over and over again during the next half hour, each woman citing personal examples of humiliating confrontations with her husband. Most of them had their own checking accounts, but their spending options were as circumscribed as those described by Graciela. Thus, in the final analysis, they were beholden to their respective spouses and inevitably had to rely on all sorts of guile—tearful pleas, pathetically empty threats, prolonged pouting, sexual refusals, devious accountings, and spasms of real anger.

"And every time we pull that crap," said Rachel, "we lose another fraction of personal esteem and finally start to hate ourselves. Some call it self-pity, but it's really self-hate."

"But what can we do about it?"

"Start earning our own money. Get outside jobs. Put our kids in day care centers." It was Graciela rattling off suggestions in short breathless phrases. "Become more independent."

"Easier said than done."

"Well, I'm certainly going to try, Jan. I'm also going back into teaching, even though I've been away from it for twelve years. And my husband will have to do his share of the damned housekeeping."

"Do you think he will?"

"I frankly don't know. But he won't get any dinner unless he does. And I certainly won't do his damned laundry."

163

"That poor Chicano's going to rebel," said Rachel teasingly.

"This Chicana already has," responded Graciela. "It's been boiling inside me for a long long time. I'm sorry I waited till now."

They all agreed (with varying degrees of self-persuasion) that outside jobs were the *sine qua non* of true economic independence for married women and that their husbands would have to share the household chores, but when the initial euphoria of anticipated rebellion had simmered down, there were some misgivings.

"First of all," said Selma, "we've got to get our kids into this action, and that won't be easy at my house. Take Shari, for example. Aside from being periodically bitchy, she's lazy, sloppy, careless, and just charming enough with daddy to get away with most of her shit. As for Sid and Jerry, they're even sloppier and lazier. So I'm not so sure I'd want them helping me in the kitchen or making their own goddamned meals. I can already visualize the horrible mess my stove would be with the spillovers from every pot and pan I've got, and the floor piling up with all the garbage and trash that always seems too damned heavy to carry over to the disposal bags. . . ."

"So why don't you just leave it there until they themselves clean it up?"

"I've tried it, sweetie. Two or three times a month I try that strategy. But it finally gets so friggin messy—so awful damned cruddy, especially in the summertime, when the flies get into the scene—that I finally put on a gas mask and clean it up myself. Or I call the employment service for a maid. Then, because I can't stand the embarrassment of someone else looking at my kitchen, I take off for the day. For a double-feature movie or maybe the art museum. And I'll leave an apologetic note with a check attached, paying her double time to salve my conscience. So I'm not so sure I can stand the necessary changes we've been talking about. . . ."

She paused as if to absorb the impact of her own ever-escalating doubts, then continued in a voice tinged with an oh-so-weary acceptance of the unacceptable.

"But even if my kids were clean and helpful, I still can't do a thing about all the goddamned rituals that force all of us into that old mommy bag. We're being ritualized every minute of the day—by television, radio, newspapers, and everything else."

"What kind of rituals?"

"All those damned good-mommy rituals that come at us from all directions. Mommy showing daughter how to use lemon wax polish, mommy telling daughter what coffee to use, mommy and daughter using the same detergent, mommy taking Nitol so she can be a nicer mommy, mommy serving daddy the right kind of beer so he can sit on his fat ass all weekend watching football, mommy forever smiling as everybody gives her a royal screwing. Every other commercial promotes that lousy myth. And the terrible irony—the really awful thing about that perpetual message—is that most of us are accepting it. And I include myself. Because no matter how much I sneer, I occasionally catch myself imitating those damned sweet smiling mommies—and . . . well . . . you're not going to believe this—but I'm secretly pleased when Shari asks me to show her how to make an apple pie with the dough mix she's seen advertised on TV."

"And of course Shari is imitating that television daughter," Rachel added.

"She sure is," agreed Selma. "We're both buying that mother-daughter myth. We're acting out a ritual that's centuries old."

"But what's wrong with that?" asked Jan.

"Well, first of all, it freezes us into a mold that's

165

totally restrictive, that makes us suppress and deny all kinds of abilities and natural drives. And if you want to break that mold, you're automatically considered a neurotic, ungrateful bitch."

"Not necessarily, Selma."

"Okay, Jan—just try it once. Violate one of those sacred mother rituals, and see what happens. As a matter of fact, I've just thought of an excellent idea. But you'll have to wait until Thanksgiving Day to try it out."

"Maybe I will. Now, what's your idea?"

"Well, instead of serving your family a turkey dinner, just give them a meat loaf—preferably a frozen one that you can stick in the oven."

"But that's crazy!" exclaimed Jan. "I couldn't do that. They'd think I was crazy."

"Of course they would, sweetie. Because that whole turkey scene is about the most *sacred* and *feminine* ritual we have in this country."

"But it's not strictly a female thing," Ruth protested. "It's a whole family ritual."

"Like hell it is!" said Rachel. "It's a female thing from beginning to end. Selma is dead right on this one. It's mommy all the way. We do all the shopping because papa's supposed to be too dumb to get the right turkey and the right cranberries and the right everything else. Then we do all that damned cooking and baking the ritual homemade pies and biscuits like mama used to make them, and setting the table with just the right candles and centerpiece, and (just in case we ain't busy enough) we're rushing back and forth to make sure our menfolk have enough cold beer and little tidbits to stuff their goddamned bellies while they watch their football games. And you'd better not forget those special cranberries—or any other detail of that ritual, honey—because someone is going to bitch about it and remind you

166

that *his* mommy never forgot! So don't tell me Thanks-giving isn't a female ritual."

"Even so," said Jan, "I'm still serving turkey."

"So am I," said Rachel. "I'm just as hung up on that turkey ritual as anyone else. But this year my husband's doing all the shopping. And he also has to promise to wash all the pots and pans."

"What if he doesn't?"

"Then I'll serve him a frozen pizza, and I'll take the kids to a fancy restaurant."

"And who would pay for it?"

"Well, I'd get the money one way or another," answered Rachel, hints of humor sliding into her previously petulant voice. "I might act a mother bit for one of those TV commercials. Or if worse comes to worse, I could always hustle a little sex. As a matter of fact, we could all earn a few bucks that way."

Spasms of choked laughter and a few giggles trailed after her suggestion; then Graciela added a further comment.

"That's not as crazy as it sounds, Rachel. In fact, it's already been done. By that group of wives who lived in Long Island. . . ."

"In my old hometown," Isabel interjected, "I re-member reading about them a couple of years ago. They were strictly daytime prostitutes, mostly in the early afternoon while their kids were still in school."

"Were they actually mothers?"

"They sure were, Ruthie. They were white middle-class mommies, whose husbands had very respectable jobs. In fact, most of their husbands knew about it and never objected."

"You're kidding."

"Not according to what I read," said Isabel. "Those wives were earning extra money to help pay the mort-

167

gages on their typical suburban homes, so their husbands thought it was okay."

"But how could they do such a thing?"

"Well, now that you've asked that crucial question," said Selma, mockingly lowering and hollowing her voice to a proper solemn-judge level, "I'm sure that a careful investigation will clearly show that those Long Island wives had originally met with each other for consciousness-raising sessions. . . ."

"And one thing led to another," added Rachel. "I wonder what will. . . ."

Breaking into the discussion as someone else started to talk, Rachel stunned the others into an awkward silence with unconcealed sarcasm in her throaty voice. "I'm sure feeling sorry for us poor suburban chicks—I really am. But just now, as I was fixin' to shed a few tears for us, I got to thinking about all my black sisters in the ghetto, all those black women you see walking to the bus stops and suburban train stations after taking care of our housecleaning once or twice a week, dragging their fannies 'cause they been doin' the real messy and heavy work that we leave for them. And carrying their tote bags—those brown paper sacks that cause so much curiosity and suspicion among the white ladies who hire them. But I had an aunt back in Chicago—Auntie Lu—who was too proud to carry anything so ordinary and common as a paper sack. No, siree, Auntie Lu had herself a fancy oilskin shopping bag from Sears, Roebuck. And that caused a mess of trouble for her one day. This lady she cleaned for on Thursdays got to thinking Auntie Lu was taking things now and then. Well, one afternoon Mrs. Wilson couldn't find one of her favorite bracelets, so right in front of two neighbor ladies, she told Auntie Lu to open her bag and pour everything on the kitchen table. And when she didn't find the bracelet—nothing really, except a pair of work slippers and some rubber

168

gloves my Auntie always carried with her to protect her hands—this old bitch made her take off her sweater, her dress, and her damned shoes for what she called a real close inspection. And in the middle of all that shit, Mrs. Wilson's teen-age kid came into the kitchen wearing the goddamned bracelet."

"Oh, my God," someone said in a husky whisper.

"And after all that humiliation, that bitch didn't even apologize to Auntie Lu. But the worst part of it all—the thing that drove me up the wall when she told mama about it—was that she went on working for that scum. 'Because I have to,' she said. 'Because they ain't too much work—and she always gives me her old clothes at Christmas.' . . . Well, anyway, I couldn't help thinking about all that when someone mentioned that business of leaving the kitchen mess for the day worker and running off to a matinee movie, leaving a check for double time because everything had gotten so putrid and smelly—because I can almost bet that the person who cleaned the mess was a black woman."

"You'd win that bet," said Selma meekly. "I'm the one who did that, Rachel. And you're making me feel awful guilty."

"Didn't mean to, sweetie. I wasn't signaling you out. I also leave a big mess for my once-a-week maid. Except that I always try to hire white women. If I can get one who'll stay once she finds out I'm black. But coming from my kind of background, I still feel uncomfortable hiring someone to do my dirty work."

"So do I," said Graciela. "I guess you might call it ghetto guilt."

"But you've never lived in a ghetto," said Trudy. "I remember your telling us that you grew up in a middle-class neighborhood."

Graciela acknowledged that fact, chuckling slightly as she pointed out that it was middle class by Chicano standards. "But my folks really were from a poor *barrio*. My mother grew up in that section of Monterey that John Steinbeck wrote about in *Cannery Row*. She and all her sisters—four of them—worked in canning factories from the time they were teen-agers, none of them finishing school. But mom was always changing from one job to another because the foremen (and sometimes the bosses themselves) were always trying to get sexy with her. She was awfully pretty and had a nice figure (I've seen pictures of her), so, naturally, all these men were after her. But knowing how jealous her boyfriend was—he later became my dad—she wouldn't give them the time of day. Yet they'd still keep trying, and she'd finally get a job somewhere else."

"How about her sisters?"

"Well, they weren't quite as pretty, so they had fairly steady jobs."

"That sure sounds familiar," said Jan with a reminiscent sigh, remembering her three years as a waitress in several diners. "I started working nights during my last year in high school—when my dad got hurt in an accident that laid him up for almost a year—and I had to change jobs every two or three months. It was either the boss or one of the fry cooks—someone always trying to devirginize me. I guess I had that look. . . ."

"I can well imagine," said Graciela.

"I 'specially hated closing time, when all the customers were gone. That's when the boss would ask me to help him with some stupid thing that would keep me there till all the cooks had gone. Then came the old Romeo bit. First a little touch here, then one there (always accidental, of course), then the big lunge like a damned teen-age football player. And me fighting him off as nice as I could, so I wouldn't get him too sore and lose my job. But after a while, when they realized they'd have to rape me to get into my pants, they'd either leave me alone or fire me—and most of the time it was firing me."

"How about the customers? Did they ever make passes?"

"All the time. But that didn't bother me, 'cause there was always a counter between us. And if you put them off, what could they do? They sure couldn't fire you. And if they quit tipping you or just gave you a measly dime, you gave them warmed-over coffee or stale bread. . . . Then one day Ron came in—"

"Your husband?"

"My *future* husband."

"That's what I meant, Jan—your future husband. But what made him different from the rest?"

"Well, I guess he was more stubborn. He wouldn't quit. He kept trying to date me. Two or three times a week he'd ask me. So I finally gave in. But I wouldn't let him touch me—I mean, not in a sexy way. Just a lotta necking. Then he finally married me. Because—like he always said—I was an honest-to-God virgin."

Sighing heavily, as if she had heard every possible variation of the same story, Graciela wearily surmised that "he probably wouldn't have married you if you'd let him get you in bed before then."

"You're probably right, Grace. He definitely wanted a virgin. It's that Italian *macho* thing. Just like your Mexicans. And after they marry you, the whole thing changes. The sex may go on for a while, but the romance goes out the window. You become a maid with extra obligations. And he keeps you in your place by the power of the purse. So that even as a waitress I had more independence—a lot poorer, but much more independent. My virginity was my bargaining power, my only bargaining power. And after that was gone—well. . . ."

171

IX

Males Rapping

ON a Friday morning in late September, John received a phone call from Ruth's husband, Dr. Walter Kane. After the usual thirty-second delay which so many secretaries contrive to create the impression that their bosses are perpetually tied up on long distance, the call was relayed through the intercom:

"John, this is Walter. How've you been?"

"Fine, Walter, just fine. And you?"

"Nothing to complain about," was the expected reply. "I'm wondering if we could have lunch today at the club. Something I'd like to discuss with you."

"I'm sure I can, John. Let me. . . . Yep, my calendar's clear. You name the time."

"How about twelve fifteen—at the University Club? And I'd like to bring one of my colleagues. Okay?"

"Fine. I'll see you then."

Though he had briefly speculated about the reason for the sudden invitation, John thought little about it until he was on his way to the club. Kane and he had never lunched together, but they had occasionally shared a drink after a round of golf at the Cheshire Club, chatting indifferently about their scores. So he had no inkling of what Kane wished to discuss. Certainly something more serious than politics or golf. Perhaps his inclusion of a fellow doctor was the clue. Of course!

That's what it was: They had heard of his recent acquisition of a minor interest in a major pharmaceutical firm. Perhaps they had invented a new drug for menopause or hemorrhoids. Well, he'd soon find out.

Kane and his colleague were waiting at a table near the heavily draped french window at the far side of the dining room, both rising to greet him as the maître d' led him to their table.

"John, old man—good to see you," said Kane with an appropriate smile. "I'd like you to meet Dr. Gordon—Wesley Gordon—one of my partners in that medical center I built last year."

They exchanged the usual pleasantries, and all three ordered scotch and water. John casually studied their faces as they ordered and later described them as "cut from the same cloth—lean, well tanned and carefully groomed, with the cool confident precision one associates with successful WASP's." They were both about forty-five.

"I realize you're on a tight schedule, John," said Kane after the drinks arrived. "So I'd like to get down to the reason I called you. It's about our wives and those rap sessions they've been having. Wesley's wife is also involved—but in a different group."

"Go ahead," said John, fingering his cold glass. "I'm listening, Walter."

"Well, to put it bluntly, my wife came home after their meeting Thursday night and told me she wanted a divorce. Just like that. No prior discussion about it—no preliminaries of any kind. Just a cold, flat announcement."

"And I see the same thing coming at my house," said Gordon. "These damned rap sessions have completely fucked up my marriage. I don't even recognize Wanda anymore. She's like a stranger."

173

"I'm not surprised," said John, his stomach suddenly queasy. "I guess they've all changed quite a bit. Mine certainly has."

"Anyway, John, let me explain why I've wanted to chat with you." Kane took a quick sip and then proceeded. "I've heard Ruth calling your wife several times lately, almost always isolating herself in the sewing room when the conversation gets going. So, of course, I haven't known what the hell they're talking about. . . ."

"And you're wondering if I've heard anything on our end of the line."

"Precisely, John—because, damn it, I'd like to know why in hell she wants this damned divorce all of a sudden."

"Well, I wish I could help you, Walter. But my wife always drags the phone into her dressing room when it's something personal. And during these past few months *every* call seems personal—except the ones I get."

"I got the same deal at my house," mumbled Gordon, staring at his glass.

"Well, I can't afford a divorce right now," said Walter quite emphatically. "It would foul up a couple of tax shelters I've gotten involved in. Otherwise, I'd say to hell with it . . . and maybe shack up with my office manager."

"Now that would be nice," observed Gordon, momentarily lifted from his gloom. "She's a real looker, Walter. Wouldn't mind slicing a little of that tissue for myself."

"It's even nicer than you think," Walter bragged with a slight snicker. "And she doesn't hassle me with all that feminist crap I've been getting from Ruth. She enjoys being a damned female."

"So does my lab technician," said Gordon. "We spent almost a week together at our convention in

174

Miami, and I didn't hear a single damned word about male chauvinist pigs."

"Yeah—but I keep wondering what they'd be like if you married one of them. . . ."

They continued speculating in that vein and comparing experiences at past conventions and alleged "fishing trips" for about ten minutes, John meanwhile wondering how their respective wives would rate them on the "male chauvinist scale" (ten? nine? eight?) and inwardly concluding that his score might be a couple of points closer to the zero ideal than theirs. Nevertheless, he still shared their resentment of what he considered "our wives' more blatant accusations of *machismo*." Gordon, for example, complained bitterly about his wife's newborn conviction that he had performed numerous hysterectomies that had been totally unnecessary, simply because he secretly hated women.

"Now if you buy that line of shit, I might as well quit my fuckin' practice. Where would she get that radical crap?"

"From those other gals," said Kane. "And from all this feminist literature that's been flooding the market. . . . Have you seen this new magazine called *Ms*? Just read a couple of pages, Wesley—it'll make you vomit. Worse than any Communist rag. And a helluva lot more dangerous."

"Does Ruth subscribe?"

"She did. But I've burned every goddamned issue that's been delivered. I won't stand for any of that crap in my house."

"Is it sexy?" asked Wesley.

"You mean like *Playboy*?"

"Yeah."

"Hell, no! *Playboy*'s funny, Wesley. This *Ms* is sick, I mean sick-sick. And you should see the fuckin' vulgar language those gals are using. Make you vomit."

175

"You mean like 'shit' and 'fuck'—that sort of thing."

"Worse than that, buddy. And I'll tell you something else: My own wife has started to use those words. . . ."

"So do my kids," John interjected, but apparently went unheard as Kane's voice rose a few decibels.

"And you've got to remember she was a Sunday school teacher until a few years ago, when she suddenly stopped going to church altogether. Here I am, the head deacon for nearly ten years, and my own wife drops out. But the worst part is her language. First she starts with a few 'damns' now and then, sort of self-consciously. Then suddenly she springs 'bitches' on me, referring to her own mother as 'one of those awful *bitches.*' "

"You're kidding me, Walter. Not Ruthie."

"Well, after that, the word 'shit' came pretty easy to her. And any minute now I'm expecting to hear her telling me to fuck myself. Just like that . . . and when I stop to think about how and where we met, I really can't believe all this is happening."

"Where *did* you meet?" asked John, having apparently forgotten that Ruth had mentioned it on the very first tape recording.

"We met at a church supper and got married at that very same church a year later."

"Are you still attending the same church?"

"No—that was back in Iowa. Where I attended medical school and served my internship while Ruth was teaching in elementary school. Boy, was she a different gal then."

"So was Wanda," said Gordon wistfully. "She worked her ass off while I was interning in Chicago. And her old man helped us a little. But they all get bitchy, I guess, even the best of 'em. Though she's still pretty clean on the language bit. 'Shit' is about as far as she'll go. But only when she's really pissed off. My two teen-age daughters are something else. They both sound like little chippies. Maybe worse."

"Mine does, too," said John. "How about your kids, Walter?"

"Don't have any, thank the good Lord. But maybe Ruth would be better off if we did. She wouldn't have time for all this Women's Lib crap." He paused and looked out the window, musing almost inaudibly. "She had this female problem . . . in her uterus. So we didn't try for any kids, although she took several tests at. . . ."

Listening to Kane's rambling discourse on her organic disability, John suddenly remembered Ruth's contrary explanation for their not having children. She had reluctantly revealed on the sixth tape that it was Walter who was sterile, who had gone to the Mayo Clinic for hormone injections and sperm counts. And though she had seemed terribly shy and troubled, she had also been more exact, more convincing, than her husband.

"So maybe, it's just as well," Kane was saying as the waiter handed him the luncheon check. "I wouldn't want to risk raising kids with all this permissiveness that's going around like some new disease."

"That's what it is," Gordon agreed. "It's really a disease. And there's no kind of surgery to get rid of it. My lousy kids give me nothin' but problems. You take my son now—he's only sixteen—but I don't know what to do with him."

"What's the problem, Gordon?"

"The usual shit. Pot, hash, and every damned pill you can think of. He uses my goddamn uppers more than I do—steals 'em out of my bathroom. And then he goes prancing around like some damn queer. Not that he's really queer, mind you—but he puts on this act just to annoy me." His voice trailed off as if another worry had crossed his mind, his eyes fixed on the crystal salt shaker in front of him. "But Wanda doesn't seem to give a damn—I mean about this damn queer act that Larry puts on. She was telling me the other night that there's nothing wrong with people being homosexual and accused me of having this hangup about queers. Which isn't so, you know. I couldn't care less what anybody does with his private sex life—as long as it's not someone in my own family. I mean, who wants his son to be a goddamn fag?"

"You mean your wife wouldn't care if Larry really was sort of homosexual?"

"Now, just a minute, Walter, I'm not saying he's that way, because I know he's only putting on this act to annoy me, the way kids do these days—anything to bug the old man. But what I'm saying is this: that Wanda wouldn't care if he *was* a fag. It's part of this new permissive kick that she's getting from all this Women's Lib crap, and from all the stuff she reads in that *Ms* magazine. You should see the articles in favor of lesbianism in that rag."

Walter smiled knowingly as they got up from the table and prepared to leave the dining room. "I guess Ruth's been getting the same line of crap on the lesbian business. That's part of our problem these days."

"How so?"

"Well, we've never been too active about sex. We do it all right, but it's no big thing to Ruth. She can take it or leave it, and I don't press it too much, because, after all, I've still got this steady deal with my office manager."

"Yeah, she's all right, Walter. You've really got a live one there. Good-looking, too."

"But anyway," said Walter, pausing to accept Gordon's approval and glancing at John for double confirmation, "Ruth has been on this new slant lately, the lesbian thing I mentioned. She keeps defending the whole idea whenever the problem pops up—like in one of those David Suskind shows where a bunch of dykes get

178

on camera and start proposing that all women get into the lesbian act, and Ruth sits there agreeing with them."

"She does? She really does?"

"Which is all right," continued Walter, impatiently ignoring the intrusion. "She's entitled to her goddamned opinions, so long as she keeps them to herself—just between her and the TV set. But I really get pissed off when she starts that nonsense when we're at a party with some of the doctors at my medical center, spouting off about any one woman being free to do as she pleases with her sex life. It's the same nonsense that's printed in all this Women's Lib literature, especially that *Ms* magazine."

Kane was still ranting against the magazine when they got into the elevator and rode down to the street level, where they quickly parted company and took off in separate directions. On his way back to the office, still thinking about their medical metaphors for almost any personal relationship, John detoured through a hotel lobby and purchased a copy of *Ms* at the magazine counter. He had occasionally glanced at a page or two of his wife's regularly delivered copy, but now he promised himself to read it from cover to cover.

X

Divorce—Before and After

Men always want to be a woman's first love. That is their clumsy vanity. Women have a more subtle instinct about things: what they like is to be a man's last romance.

—OSCAR WILDE,
A Woman of No Importance

HAVING overheard a few guarded remarks by his wife during several of her phone conversations with other women, John soon came to the conclusion that Ruth had taken the first step in filing a divorce action against Walter. She had apparently seen two attorneys from different law firms, the first one having impressed her as being "too darned priggish and probably antifeminist."

"He sat behind that big desk, staring at me with his sharp critical eyes," she later told the group at their regular Thursday night session. "Even before I had finished telling my reasons for wanting a divorce, he started asking me a lot of—well, I guess you'd have to call them hostile questions. Yes, that's what they were all right—hostile. As if he were actually cross-examining me.

"For example, when I told him we had no children, he immediately asked me why I didn't want them. And when I explained that Walter had this physical problem that made it impossible to have kids, he muttered

180

something under his breath and stared out the window, clamping his thin lips together as if to hold back a nasty remark. . . ."

"Perhaps he's also impotent."

"That did occur to me, Rachel. But then I realized he was pretty negative about everything. In fact, he finally asked me if I had another man in my life and quite obviously doubted me when I told him I'd never in my life had an affair."

"How about Walter?"

"Oh, I doubt that, Selma. Sex has never seemed that important to him."

"But haven't you ever been tempted, Ruth?"

"Well, that's what the first lawyer asked me. But I didn't think it was any of his business, so I just lied to him. . . . Actually, I've been tempted two or three times. One of them was the minister of our church, Roscoe Pendleton, who got transferred four or five years ago. We had this sneaky little flirtation when I was in the choir, but it never got beyond a few wild kissing sessions in his office. And that's when I quit going to church. I felt so guilty and hypocritical that I couldn't face anyone connected with that place. With my kind of uptight church background, I guess that entire episode made me feel like a whore—like one of those Long Island wives you were talking about last week. And the reason I was asking Isabel all those questions was that I—well, I . . . I guess it's not too important really."

"Go ahead and tell us, Ruth. Everything's important. Especially if it bothers you."

"Okay then. Here's what I was going to say. About the time I broke away from Roscoe, I saw this Late Late Movie on TV about this prostitute who had an affair with a preacher, in some place like Tahiti.* And I found

* Probably *Miss Sadie Thompson*, starring Rita Hayworth and José Ferrer.

myself totally sympathizing with that woman. Well, after that I started having this strange dream in which I was a secret prostitute who specialized in having affairs with Protestant ministers—and no one else. . . ."

"That's beautiful," said Rachel in a half whisper that could have been mocking or dead serious.

"And I still have that dream now and then," Ruth continued. "Which sometimes worries me. I keep wondering if there's something basically evil in my nature."

"I wouldn't worry about it," said Selma. "There are a lot of women who subconsciously imagine themselves as prostitutes. Have you ever noticed—when there's a costume party—how many women come dressed as Sadie Thompson?"

"You're talking about me," said Rachel. "I've dressed like her at least twice—net stockings, strapped shoes, fur piece, and the whole bit."

"So have I," admitted Graciela. "And my uptight husband got mad as hell at me, then deliberately avoided me all night. He was particularly annoyed with the low neck on my dress, telling me that I looked like a damned whore. So when I told him that's exactly how I wanted to look, he gave me the big freeze."

"But I never look that way in *my* dreams," said Ruth somewhat defensively. "I just look like me. Like a middle-class suburban wife—without any sex appeal."

"That's where you're wrong, Ruthie. Those Long Island wives you mentioned—the ones who were arrested for prostitution—well, they all looked like middle-class suburban housewives, and that's what made them so attractive. They gave their customers the illusion of having real love affairs—instead of something crassly commercial. That's why fancy call girls can charge more. Because they don't look like whores. . . . Incidentally, there's one thing I forgot to mention about those Long Island wives. One of them started making more money than her husband—a lot more because her earnings were tax free—and that naturally caused problems with him. He didn't mind her being a matinee prostitute, but it hurt his *machismo* when she became the chief breadwinner and. . . ."

Roars of appreciative laughter blotted out her voice. Then Trudy started telling a story which John had heard in the locker room at his golf club.

"And that reminds me of the suburban couple who were having severe financial problems because the husband had lost his job at IBM. They struggled along on practically nothing for several weeks, and finally the wife said, 'I'll just have to go to work.' Sneering at her, he said, 'What the hell can you do? You've never had a job.' Naturally, that got her mad. 'I'll become a prostitute,' she said. 'Any woman can do that.' So they argued back and forth, but he finally consented. Well, that first night she spent an hour fixing her clothes and makeup like a real honest-to-God streetwalker and finally took off after feeding the kids their supper. Then eight hours later— way past midnight—she came home completely exhausted and terribly disheveled, with her dress wrinkled and soiled, her makeup rubbed off and her shoes scuffed and worn-out. 'Here's the money,' she said, putting it on the dresser. 'Forty-eight dollars and fifty cents.' 'My God!' he exclaimed. 'Who gave you the fifty cents?' And she very wearily answered, '*Everybody.*' "

Except for a couple of nervous giggles, there was a dead silence when she finished the story.

"I know I'm supposed to laugh," said Rachel. "But I couldn't even laugh the first time I heard it."

"Neither could I," said Isabel. "It sounds like such a horrible put-down for women. Why would you want to repeat it, Trudy?"

"Well, maybe I told it wrong. But I still think it's kind of funny—if you don't take it too personally."

"But how can you *not* take it personally? That's one of our sisters who is the ultimate victim—who gets laughed at."

"Oh, come on, Isabel," protested Trudy. "It's only a damned joke. She doesn't even exist, for Chrissakes!"

"Maybe *she* doesn't exist, but the idea does."

"What idea?"

"The age-old idea that women are essentially naïve and stupidly self-sacrificing. And that's all that story tells you, Trudy."

Silent for a moment, Trudy was still not ready to yield. "You're stretching this awfully far, Isabel," she finally said. "And I'm afraid we're all getting too sensitive—yes, even paranoid—if we can't take a joke like that. I really mean it. This whole feminist thing can make us awfully damned self-conscious. And I'll bet Selma will agree with me."

"Well, as far as this particular story is concerned, I'd have to agree," said Selma. "And no matter how I feel about it, you've certainly killed the joke, because there's nothing more deadly to humor than serious analysis. But, funny or not, we've strayed way off the point, so I think we'd better get back to Ruth's reaction to the two lawyers she consulted about her divorce."

Nervously clearing her throat, Ruth resumed her account in a soft tentative manner. "I knew right away I'd never be comfortable with Mr. Lewis. So the minute I got back to Westlake, I called his office and told him not to file any papers, that I had changed my mind. And he gave me this smug little laugh. 'I knew you would,' he said. 'I guess you finally realized that you're a lot better off than most women.' Which made me awfully angry—I mean his casual assumption that he'd made me see the light."

"And when did you see the second attorney?"

"The very next day. And Mr. Branton was totally

different. He put me at ease right off the bat. 'You don't have to tell me anything personal about yourself or your marriage,' he said. 'All I have to know is the vital statistics—date of marriage, the age and names of any children, and a list of personal and real property. But I'm perfectly willing to listen to anything else you want to say.' And when I asked him what reasons I'd have to give for wanting a divorce, he said, 'We'll just cite the usual abstract reasons. There's no point in getting personally nasty or vindictive on either side. People don't have to become permanent enemies just because they can't make it as husband and wife.' So I didn't have to tell him that we don't have kids because Walter is impotent. And I didn't have to say anything bad about him, anything personal. Which made me feel a lot better—and, curiously, a lot more mature. That other attorney had kind of forced me into a bitchy role. But Mr. Branton was just the opposite."

"Sounds pretty civilized."

"He certainly is, Trudy. And he told me that lots of divorces get needlessly nasty because the lawyers insist on dragging out all the dirty family linen in open court, reviving old forgotten angers, that should never be public. 'Consequently,' he said, 'my clients make only the most minimal complaint—just enough to satisfy the legal requirements.' That's all."

"So what will it be? I mean your complaint at the actual court hearing?"

"Well, according to Mr. Branton, I'll testify that Walter sometimes criticized my cooking in front of my friends, and that it made me nervous and upset my stomach."

"And that's grounds for divorce?"

"That's what he says. And he's handled lots of cases."

"Oooh, my God," said Selma with a heavy reminiscent sigh. "I sure wish my parents had been represented by lawyers like Branton. They had a terrible divorce. I've never heard anything so nasty, so full of hate and venom. They tore into each other like rabid dogs, accusing each other of the most horrible things, each dirty detail of their marriage getting the fullest exposure, so that they were finally stripped of any personal dignity. And my brother and I—twelve and fourteen years old—sat in that damned courtroom dying of shame and anguish, wanting to run away forever. We had of course heard them fight that way at home—perhaps using fouler language—but watching the same act in a public courtroom, I thought it was unforgivably obscene.

"And yet they finally got together again before the decree was final, but I don't think either one ever forgot what they had said in that courtroom. I certainly never forgot. In fact, I was so traumatized that I frankly doubt that I'll ever be able to enter any divorce court—ever again. So if Alvin and I should ever decide to split, I guess he'll have to file against me, and I'll simply default."

Selma's usually strong voice had become almost inaudible, and there was a brief pause after she had stopped talking, as if she had reminded the others of countless parental squabbles in their childhood.

"My parents also had a nasty divorce," said Jan. "But the nastiness came from other reasons—at least the beginning of it. They got divorced in New York, when adultery was the only grounds for getting a divorce. And you actually had to present real proof, with photographs and witnesses. But since very few people did commit adultery—or would be willing to admit it—the lawyers had to stage these phony adultery scenes in some motel, hiring some prostitute to climb into bed with the husband, so that a private investigator and a witness could pretend to break open the door and photograph

186

the naked couple under the sheets. It was phony and stupid, but the damned courts demanded that kind of evidence. . . ."

"Was it always the husband getting caught?"

"That's what I've been told, Ruth. It was the man. So when my folks decided to split up (I was about twelve then), it was my dad who very reluctantly posed for one of those fake pictures. But even after they'd gotten divorced—years later—my mother still used them against him."

"The fake photos?"

"That's right, Rachel. She'd gotten three copies from the investigator, and whenever she'd get into an argument with dad about visitation rights or back alimony, she'd start calling him a goddamned whore chaser. 'And I've got photographs to prove it!' she'd yell, obviously trying to influence me and my brothers. 'They caught you in bed with that peroxide chippy, and I've got pictures of it.' And when he'd start to explain, she'd yell right over his voice, screaming and threatening to show us the pictures. So I didn't really know the truth until I'd gotten married myself."

"Did she ever show you the photos?"

"No, she didn't. But I saw them anyway," said Jan with a slight break in her voice. "She had mentioned them so often that I finally had to see them. My curiosity was—well, you can imagine what I mean. So one Saturday afternoon, when mom was out shopping with my Aunt Maire, I sneaked into her bedroom and searched through back shelves in her closet and found this big manila envelope. But I didn't open it right away. I sat on her bed, with the envelope on my lap, fingering the loose flaps and wondering if I should really look inside. Because I knew—I had this awful feeling—that the photos were there. Finally, after agonizing for at least ten minutes, I took out the photos and stared at them.

187

Sure enough, there was my dad snuggled under the sheets with a fat frizzy-haired blonde who had this Mickey Mouse watch on her wrist. Sitting there with those blow-up photos in my hand, I wanted to vomit and to tear them into a thousand bits and pieces and flush everything down the john. I've never felt so sick and sad. Never. Because I'd always sort of worshiped him in spite of all the nasty things mom had told us about him—most of which I knew were lies or exaggerations. But how could those photos lie? . . . And the strangest part of it all, the really screwy part, was my reaction to that cheap watch she was wearing. Somehow, that kind of cheapness and the awful emptiness of that motel room, with those bare walls and the cheap lamp on the Sears, Roebuck table—that whole shoddy scene—made it all the more sickening and totally vulgar."

"Would you have felt better if he'd been photographed with a high-class call girl in an expensive fancy bedroom?"

"Well . . . I guess this will sound snobbish on my part, but I'll have to admit that I would probably feel better. It would still hurt me, though maybe in a different way. Because with that kind of setup, you might possibly imagine that he was with someone he really loved—not just a whore. *That* I could somehow understand, particularly when you considered what a bitch my mother could be, and how any other fairly nice woman would naturally appeal to him."

"How old were you?"

"When?"

"At the time you saw the photos?"

"Just past sixteen—about a month after my birthday, when my dad had given me all kinds of wonderful gifts, and we had eaten a fantastic dinner at my favorite Chinese restaurant. He'd even let me sip his daiquiri. . . . But we didn't have dinner together again for a long,

188

long time. I couldn't stand to be alone with him anymore. No matter how nice and friendly he was. I just couldn't get those pictures out of my mind—that cheap blonde with her damned Mickey Mouse watch. So after a while he stopped mentioning lunch or dinner, and we'd go out as a group whenever he came for his weekly visitation with me and my younger brothers—maybe to the beach or a bowling alley or someplace equally impersonal.

"Then about eight years later, when I was about twenty-four and already married to Ron, one of my girlfriends was getting divorced, and I went with her to the lawyer's office. And that's when I found out about the fake photos that were used to prove adultery. It hit me like a sledgehammer, and I ran out of that office crying like a baby, hating myself for the way I'd snubbed my dad and hating my mother a lot worse for being such a shitty mean bitch. So that same afternoon I called him and asked him to have dinner with me. Alone. At my old favorite Chinese place—which I'd never gone back to. And with big tears gushing down my damned face, I told him everything. And then we both cried a little, hiding our faces behind the big menu. But what he said afterward, while we were cracking open the fortune cookies, that really got to me. He said, 'Please don't start hating your mother, Jan. You've got to understand how desperate people can get when their marriage has gone sour and all their dreams have been shattered. I guess when you've been hurt a lot, you want to hit back. And the more defenseless you feel, the harder you hit. So don't blame her too much.' Then he hugged me and thanked me for letting him know why I'd suddenly started to avoid him. 'It's nice to know that it wasn't a case of bad breath or maybe body odor,' he said. So now we have lunch at least once a month."

"Did you ever tell your mother about the photos?"

189

"Nope. I never did. I had to agree with my dad when he said it was better to let sleeping dogs lie. He knew that was an old cliché, but it was one of his favorite proverbs. . . . Anyway, that's why I'm so afraid of poisoning my kids' minds against my husband. Because it always hurts *them* more than him. And there's also the danger of a bitchy wife eventually becoming a bitch period. I saw it happen with my mother."

"That's so true," said Graciela. "That so-called bitch syndrome can be awfully contagious. And that's what worries me about some of the Women Libbers I've seen on television. They're so full of hate against all men. And I can't buy that. Take, for example, our own fathers. During the past few months we've all mentioned our dads in one way or another, and I've gotten the impression that most of them were fairly decent men. Weak at times, possibly ignorant about certain things, but generally well intentioned. Whereas our mothers have so frequently come off as frantic and pretty bitchy. And, quite frankly, I'm afraid most of our kids get the same impression."

"Of course they do," snapped Rachel. "We probably are bitchier. Because we're on the front lines getting most of the shit and therefore having more to bitch about."

"And just as Jan's father told her, we're more defenseless and probably more desperate," said Graciela. "That's because we've become so dependent on our husbands, economically and psychologically. Which is one of the scarier aspects of getting a divorce—that economic dependence on a man who is bound to resent every cent he gives you. And you're suddenly trapped with less money and almost the same household bills, the same food bills, the same mortgage payments, medical bills, clothing bills, the same everything. . . ."

"Except liquor bills," interjected Jan.

190

"Except liquor bills," said Graciela, absentmindedly repeating the words. "But she's got all the same expenses with slightly more than half as much money. Both of them, husband and wife, trying to run two households on the same amount of money they had before. Much less, in fact, because of all the lawyer's fees and court costs. Consequently, it's a month-to-month worry about that damned check for child support and alimony, and fretting about the husband forgetting to send it in time or deliberately holding it back to teach you a lesson. And then the humiliating phone call to remind him, to beg him, not to forget—or the final angry sarcasm and bitchiness when you realize he's simply being a bastard, and somehow hating the money because it's his and because you've had to beg for it. Then the scrimping and cutting corners and telling your kids they can't have this or that, when you're dying to give them any guilt offering to salve your conscience for getting rid of their father."

"How about the divorced husband, Graciela? It's also rough on him."

"Of course it is, Jan. And I was coming to that. In fact, I was just thinking about my own brother. He's got a darned good job in broadcasting, and he and his wife and three kids had this wonderful house on a half acre of land with a three-car garage and all that stuff. But after a long expensive custody battle, they had to sell the house, and she's renting a smaller one. Meanwhile, Humberto has moved into this furnished apartment that depresses the hell out of him—and anyone else who sees it. There's nothing, but nothing at all, that's homey or personal about it. No bookshelves, no paintings, no pre-Columbian artifacts like the ones he had in the house, nothing that tells you who's living there. Just a bleak vacant apartment that looks like a way station to nowhere. And because he hates to eat alone, there's nothing in his refrigerator except two six-packs of beer, a carton of milk, some yogurt, a frozen head of lettuce that's been there since God knows when, and a frozen pizza he'll probably never eat. And his pantry has seven packages of corn-flakes, Wheaties, Cheerios, shredded wheat, and et cetera—none of which have been opened. So when he finally gets home after eating dinner and probably drinking more than he generally drank before the divorce, he sits and watches television all alone, sipping beer and piling half-smoked cigarettes on his only ashtray. . . ."

"Doesn't he ever date anyone?"

"He can't afford to. He's already spending too much just feeding himself."

"That sure sounds like my first husband's apartment after our divorce. It was so damned depressing my kid hated to go there on weekends. The only thing he liked was the frozen Mexican TV dinners. He said the pizzas were always lousy. . . ."

"But listen here," Selma interrupted. "Before you start feeling too sorry for them, just bear in mind that a divorced man has a lot more social acceptance than a divorcée has. I was separated from Alvin for almost a year, and I got a pretty good taste of what most divorced women face—particularly when they've got two or three kids. First of all, most of your married women friends begin shunning you as if you're some kind of leper. One of them may see you for lunch, but you're certainly not invited to her dinner parties. Because suddenly you're supposed to be a dangerous *femme fatale,* someone chasing after her husband. One of my oldest friends, Mary Lyons, did that to me. She cut me off completely. But her husband had already tried to approach me. Several times. The first time he came by my house around eleven in the morning, when he knew damned well the kids were in school. He told me he'd been consulting with an elderly client on the next street—on an inheritance matter—and just decided to drop by for a cup of coffee. But he was soon making an indirect pass, and I politely brushed him off. The next time he casually dropped in was on a Friday night, when all our teen-agers were at a school dance, and this time he had been drinking enough to make an out-and-out play for me, suddenly pushing me against a coatrack and clumsily trying to kiss me. But as I pulled to one side, one of my coats came loose and fell over his face. And when I wouldn't stop laughing, he got annoyed and soon left."

"Perhaps his wife knew or suspected that he was leching after you, and that's why she'd cooled on you."

"Perhaps you're right, Jan. But I sure didn't encourage him."

"It's not just a matter of encouraging him, Selma. With some men, you've actually got to *dis*courage them. Get tough. Because anything less than a violent *no* is considered a possible yes. Especially with a new divorcée. Because they all think she's dying to get laid. And they're really doing her a big favor."

"That's sure the gods' truth," Rachel quickly agreed. "My ex-husband's best friend—supposedly best friend—put it to me in exactly those terms. 'Listen, baby,' he said, 'I know what you're needing, and I got it right here.' No beating around the bush with that mother. So I came back with the only jive that will stop that kind of *machismo*. 'I'm sorry, honey,' I told him. 'But you ain't the right sex. I'd rather make it with your wife.' And that stopped him cold."

"I should think so," said Isabel. "I may try that tactic myself someday."

"But there are some men you don't want to discourage—whom you'd like to sleep with and possibly marry. But you can't when you've got kids, because they put a damper on everything. He's leary about them, because who needs that added responsibility? And

193

they're just as negative about him. Take, for example, that year I was on a trial separation from Alvin. About a month after he moved into an apartment, I met this architect (Ethan Frankel) who had once worked with Gropius. He'd been divorced about five years and was apparently happy to live alone. But we started dating quite a bit. Theater, museums, art exhibits, witty cocktail parties—the usual stuff. But whenever we got back to the house, no matter how late it might be, Shari and Larry would be sitting in the living room playing chess or writing extra book reports for better grades at school. And they'd want to read them to me. Just anything to break into any rapport I might have established with Ethan. But with such fiendish charm I couldn't put them off.

"So, as you might predict, my very eligible architect soon realized that he was caught between a teen-age son who had the usual Oedipus crush on mama and a teen-age daughter who was forever protecting her daddy's terrain. She'd mentioned him every other sentence, until I was tempted to kick her sexy little ass. Consequently, we had to go to his place for privacy and a little sex now and then. But we both eventually got tired of crawling out of bed so that he could get me home by two o'clock. The end was inevitable. He found himself a young divorcée without kids and married her six months later. And a month after that, still licking my wounds, I went back to Alvin. Thankful that he still wanted me."

"How did it feel when you got together again?"

"It was a lot better than being alone."

"But weren't your kids living with you, Selma?"

"Sure. But that's not what I'm talking about. I'm referring to this business of sleeping alone. That's what bothered me most when we were separated. Alvin and I have always cuddled in bed, curving our bodies together in different ways—especially in the fetal position—"

194

"So have we," said Jan and Rachel simultaneously. "—and that's always given me a feeling of security," said Selma. "So I really missed that snuggling when Alvin was gone. Even when I was having my fling with Ethan Frankel and two or three other men, I still had to leave their beds at two or three in the morning and go home to my own bed—go home to my empty bed with no one to snuggle. I just can't sleep alone. I keep tossing and turning and hugging my pillows, or bunching the blankets into the curve of my stomach. But no pillow can substitute for a man."

"How about a huge teddy bear?" someone suggested. "I've seen some at Orbach's."

"Believe it or not, Ruthie—I tried that. Shari got one of those stuffed bears from her Uncle Stan, and one night (pretending to the kids it was all a big joke), I took it to bed with me and tried my old snuggling act. But it didn't work—not even as well as my pillow. I had to . . ."

A sudden scraping, followed by a brief whirring screech, partially blotted her voice, as if one of the concealed microphones had suddenly been damaged or torn loose. But after a while, the interfering noises faded to a faint scratchy sound that one could easily ignore. When John and his electronic accomplice checked the apparatus on the following Tuesday afternoon, they found a few gashes in the main cord of the recording device hidden in the attic. "Probably one of the rats," said John. "Or maybe a bat. I forgot to replace the plastic cover when I changed the tapes last week."

After the initial scraping and screeching had subsided, we could hear Ruth commenting on one of the immediate consequences of her sudden decision to get a divorce. "And yesterday one of Walter's colleagues came by the house. He's a gynecologist named Bruce Hammond, who has quite a reputation for being a ladies' man. He came by at ten A.M., pretending he wanted to see Walter about an article he had written for a medical journal, although he knows Walter golfs all day on Wednesdays. 'Now that I'm here,' he said, 'I might as well discuss it with you. It's called "The Ambivalent Fetus." ' Well, I naturally thought he was kidding about the title, but he showed me the typed manuscript, and there it was—on the top of page one. So he started reading it to me as I poured him a cup of coffee, pausing now and then to make these sexy side remarks, probably testing my response to them. And when I put on my square-housewife act, he switched to a more direct approach. He suddenly grabbed me and tried to kiss me, telling me that I made him feel like a crazy schoolboy on his first date. And that's exactly how he looked. But he was so damned obvious, so well rehearsed in his sponta- neous outburst, that I started laughing at him, nearly doubling over with wild laughter and spilling my coffee all over his coat sleeve. Which got him terribly upset and angry. 'Stop pulling that innocence shit,' he said. 'You're dying for a good screw like any other dame.' Then out he went, slamming the door behind him."

"You'd better get used to that scene," observed Rachel. "And you can expect most of them will involve men you've known for a long time. I heard a similar story last week. From an old friend I hadn't seen for a long time, that college girlfriend who got me into my first lesbian affair. She's just been divorced for the second time, and now several of her husband's friends are chasing after her as if she were a bitch in heat. Including her own brother-in-law. But that's not her main problem. What worries her most is the custody battle he's still fighting against her. She got the three kids after a really nasty trial, where he accused her of laying everyone but the piano tuner. . . ."

"Why not him?"

"Because they don't have a piano—and quit interrupting me, Selma, I'm trying to be serious. I was about to tell you that her husband—still determined to get the kids by proving she's a degenerate, unfit mother—has hired a private investigator to follow her everywhere she goes and probably taking pictures of any man she talks to. And she's dead certain her phone's been tapped."

"Perhaps that's why her husband's brother is making passes at her," said Trudy. "That could be a frame-up."

"Conceivably. But Sylvia doesn't think so. Her brother-in-law has been after her for a long, long time, so he's probably serious. But it would be kind of funny if her husband should finally accuse his own brother of hanky-panky. Anyway, she's being awfully careful these days, hoping her damned husband will ultimately decide it's too expensive to keep spying on her."

"Or he might start his own spying," said Trudy, hints of bitterness in her carefully controlled voice. "That's what my father did after mom divorced him. He spied on her all the time. He bought a special camera with a long-range lens, and almost every night he'd park his car down the street from our house and shoot pictures of anyone coming or going. They were all crappy pictures, of course, because the only lighting he had was the bulb over the front door. But he took them anyway."

"How did you know he was taking them?"

"I used to see him on my way home from a date—sometimes way after midnight. And whenever I'd go visit him at this creepy apartment he lived in, I'd see the latest batch of photos on his coffee table. Some of them were barely recognizable pictures of me leaning slightly forward to press my key into the door lock. So I'd make some half-kidding remark about them, but he'd pretend not to hear me. Yet he never made any attempt to hide those damned pictures from me or my little sister.

197

He obviously wanted us to know he was taking them."

"Of course, he did. That was part of his psychological warfare. He knew damned well one of you would tell your mother, and that was a good way to spook her."

"It sure was, Rachel. She was deathly afraid of him. She hardly ever dated anyone, because she knew daddy would be lurking around somewhere. But she finally accepted a dinner invitation from an old beau she'd known in high school, a druggist who was what you'd call an old bachelor. And, sure enough, the minute they left our house my dad started following the other man's car, staying up close to him and banging his rear bumper every time they came to a stoplight. Well, after the seventh or eighth bump, mom's date spotted a police car and immediately pulled alongside to complain about what had been happening, but before the cops could catch him, dad had disappeared. So, as you can well imagine, that was the last time she dated her druggist friend.

"Then a short time later daddy began his twice-a-year court actions to get custody of me and my sister. Every six months he'd appear in court with his damned nighttime pictures, trying to convince the judge that mom was a loose woman who was dating every man in town. And I would take the stand to testify that most of the photos were blurred images of teen-age boys who had come to see me. Then one particular day—it must have been the fifth or sixth time he tried to get custody— daddy testified that some man had spent the whole night with mommy, and he showed the judge two photos of a car parked near our driveway. One was taken when it was pretty dark, and the other one showed the milkman walking past the car. But in the much lighter picture I could easily see that the car belonged to the family next door, to one of the teen-agers. And that's what I told the judge, who then scolded my dad in open court. 'You're a psychopath,' he said. 'You're a mean jealous psychopath, and I don't ever want to see you in this courthouse again.' So then my dad—"

Her voice had suddenly faded to a choked whisper, but she cleared her throat and went on in a soft but determined tone.

"So then he switched to a different tactic. He stopped sending her the monthly check for alimony and child support. Held off for three whole months. Until my mother's lawyer hauled him into court, and the judge angrily told my dad to pay all he owed in twenty-four hours or he'd send him to jail for contempt of court. But my dad stubbornly refused and sure enough got thrown into jail the following afternoon—into this big cell with all the drunks and petty thieves. His older brother, my Uncle Ralph, finally got him out by paying mom's lawyer the back payments. . . . It was so damned painful for all of us, because we knew he was sick—sick with this god-awful jealousy and loneliness. Several times I went to his creepy little apartment and begged him to be reasonable, but he would just sit there in his plastic-leather armchair and never say a word. And after a while—as if he hadn't heard anything I said—he would start talking about a movie he'd seen on the Late Late Show. Or something equally irrelevant. And I'd be choking back the tears as he talked, suddenly remembering that we had all seen the same movie before the divorce. . . .

"It's still happening," she said after another brief pause. "My husband is a lawyer—and he frequently tells me about custody battles that are just as horrible. It's always a bitter fight about children or money."

Trudy's usually crisp voice, now drained of all emotion by the painful recollection of her adolescent years, had faded to a near whisper, prompting Selma to suggest an early adjournment. "It's almost midnight," she said.

"Wait a minute," said Isabel. "I realize it's getting late, but there's something I'd like to say about psycho-analysts. It's been on my mind since we had our talk about them last month. There were lots of bitter comments that were rather unfair—at least, I think so. Particularly when I think about my own experi-ence. . . ."

She paused a few seconds as if to reconsider the pros and cons of the painful self-revelation that was to follow, stuttering at first, then proceeding in breathless haste.

"I had a nervous breakdown about five years ago, which sent me to a hospital for about five or six weeks. I don't really remember what happened there, except that it was awfully scary. Not because of any violence or craziness, but because I couldn't seem to feel any connection to anyone or anything, not even with my family when they came to visit me. But, anyway, I finally started analysis with this wonderful female clinician, whose name was Sharon Weil. She saw me during my last week at the hospital, and we continued our sessions after I got out. I mean as an outpatient at her private office.

"She was really marvelous and gentle with me, especially when I went through that awful period of what she called infantile regression."

"You mean actually going back to infancy?"

"That's right, Trudy. I went right back to the cradle. . . . First of all, I had this screwy compulsion that sort of embarrasses me even now. Anyway, I kept wanting to suck my thumb—just like a baby. I'd try to pretend that I was just biting my thumbnail whenever people were around. But that wasn't enough to satisfy the urge. So I'd suddenly rush off to the bathroom, where I could actually suck my thumb in privacy, and I might stay there five or ten minutes, hungrily mouthing both thumbs until that damned urge fizzled off. Then an hour later I'd be rushing off again."

"That must have been awful!"

"But the next phase was even more embarrassing," said Isabel. "That was the urinating phase, when I actually started wetting my pants! And the first time it happened I nearly died of shame. I was passing by the meat counter in the supermarket when I got this sudden need to tinkle, and before I could do anything about it, my panties were soaked and the urine was dribbling down the inside of both my legs. Abandoning my half-filled grocery cart, I hurried out of the store and drove home like a madwoman, looking straight ahead as if to avoid the stares of anyone I might know, certain they could see the wet blot on my skirt even though I was wearing a trench coat that undoubtedly concealed everything. So after that, for at least a week, I wore two pads of Kotex to soak up the urine that might come at any moment, also stuffing my purse with six or seven extra pads just to make sure. . . ."

"And what did Dr. Weil say about that?"

"Well, first of all, she had already warned me about this step-by-step progression through this so-called infantile regression. Even before I told her about my thumb sucking. She also said I'd get a burning sensation whenever I peed, not only in my genital organs but all through my body, and that I'd get these pounding sensations in my chest, my temples, my ears, and (worst of all) in my womb. But even with her prior warning, I wasn't quite prepared for the awful internal chaos that flushed through me—from head to toes—whenever I had to pee. My whole body got so incredibly sensitive, especially my genitals. In fact, my vaginal tissues got so sensitive the Kotex pads felt like rough canvas. But, fortunately, that urinating phase disappeared almost as abruptly as my thumb sucking. . . ."

She paused several seconds, and the sudden silence momentarily caused me to wonder if the tape had run out or had possibly been snapped off. Sitting next to me as we listened to the replay of this particular tape in Herb's office, John leaned forward and whispered, "Wait till you hear what's coming next. Really, weird." And a moment later Isabel's voice, now huskier than before, continued from where she'd left off.

"The next stage of my reversed regression—the jump from infancy to puberty, as Dr. Weil called it—was the most terrifying. And without her constant gentle reassurance that I'd live through it, that it would also finally wear off, I would have gone insane or perhaps killed myself. Anyway, just as soon as I got past that urinating binge, I suddenly got a maddening need to be penetrated. I got rid of the Kotex and went back to my Tampax, which momentarily satisfied me—but only temporarily. What I really wanted was a full-sized penis to fill that awful hungering cavity. And I wanted it constantly. The need was overpowering. The whole lower part of my body seemed to crave something . . . somebody . . . just anybody. It made no difference to my body, for it somehow seemed to be disconnected from the rest of me—starving and hungering for a purely physical sex, entirely separate from any emotional need. Consequently, any man who came near me would have been okay.
"My husband, as you might expect, got the first— what shall I call it? Impact? Assault? Challenge? I really don't know what you'd call it, but it sure knocked him for a loop. He must have thought I'd suddenly become a whore or (more likely) a nymphomaniac. I pressed and coiled around him like a bitch in heat, trying to arouse

him as he shifted away from me, finally jerking himself out of my frantic embraces, kidding me at first as if it were a silly joke, then finally getting annoyed or apprehensive. 'Jesus!' he kept saying. 'Jesus, Isabel, what the hell's gotten into you? I mean really.' And, finally, I scrambled off the bed, clenching my lips tight to hold back a scream as I ran through the hallway and rushed past the living room into the patio, where I slumped on a rubber mat that I used for sunbathing, clutching it against my body and moaning like a sick animal. I would have had sex with anyone or anything at that moment. But I settled for masturbation instead, frantically writhing, and doubling the inflated mattress between my thighs until the craving subsided to a sort of vague yearning.

"Well, after that I never bothered Big Chris anymore. I knew that I was repulsive to him, and he later accused me of embarrassing one of his colleagues while we were dancing at a neighbor's party. He said I'd given Ralph what he brutally called a dry lay on the dance floor. And perhaps he was right. I'd certainly felt sexy when his thighs were pressing against mine. In any event, I decided to avoid further contact with anyone we knew. That's when I started picking up strangers in bars at downtown hotels, hoping they would take me up to their rooms for a quickie. Sometimes I'd manage to have sex two or three times in a couple of hours—always in midafternoon, so as to get home for an early dinner with the kids—but that craving, that insatiable need, was always there. It was absolutely maddening . . . and scary as all hell. But she—I mean Dr. Weil—kept assuring me that it was temporary, that I was going through an exaggerated version of puberty, a grotesque caricature of adolescent sexuality. Those were her exact words, which I'll never forget: *a grotesque caricature of adolescent sexuality.* She put it even more plainly when she said, 'Your body is going through the pangs of a fourteen-year-old's lust, intensified by an older woman's emotional concentration.' But knowing all that didn't make it any easier. I'd still feel a crazy fever in my loins when the Negro mailman went by or when a pimply-faced kid named Billy delivered the groceries, both of whom could have taken me to bed with no effort at all.

"Then suddenly—just as Dr. Weil predicted—that siege of nymphomania came to an abrupt end, and I was my dull old self again. God, what a joy that was! To become completely unaware of your body, almost totally indifferent to men. And I could see enormous relief in Chris' eyes. But our sexual relations were never the same as before."

XI

Loneliness—Pills—
Rape—Politics

> One last plea: If we women are ever to pull ourselves out of the morass
> of self-pity, self-destruction and impotence which has been our heritage
> for so long as we can remember, then it is perhaps even more important
> that we be supportive of each other's achievements and successes and
> strengths than it is for us to be compassionate and understanding of each
> other's failures and weaknesses.
>
> ANSELMA DELL'OLIO,
> Unpublished essay

AT the beginning of the eleventh meeting
Selma announced that Jan would no longer participate
in their rap sessions.

"Her husband has given her an ultimatum—either
quit us or quit him."

"The dirty bastard," muttered Rachel. "She ought
to tell him to shove it."

"She's been considering it," said Selma. "She's been
thinking of all possible alternatives, but she's frankly
afraid of the financial problems she'd have to face."

"But Ron's wealthy," said Trudy. "He's got three
bowling alleys with a nice restaurant in each one. She'd
get plenty of alimony and child support."

"Not necessarily. According to Jan, he's heavily in
debt to a couple of Mafia types. He's been gambling a lot

and spending quite a bit on this young chippy he's been keeping in a fancy apartment. Jan first learned all this stuff a couple of weeks ago. From his cousin Phil. She had hinted to Phil that she might leave Ron, and that's when he gave her the whole messy picture."

"All the more reason to divorce him."

"Good legal reason. But not necessarily a good financial reason."

"Why not? Why stay on a sinking ship?"

"Because Phil told her that a divorce would force the whole thing into the open, and that his legitimate creditors and suppliers would close down everything. And they'd probably lose the house. But if Ron quits gambling and quits whoring around, he can still make enough income to pull himself out in a couple of years."

"What makes her so sure that he will?"

"She's not sure, Trudy. But he's promised her. They've had some pretty heavy talks about it, and Jan confronted him with everything—including some canceled checks on the chippy's rent and clothing bills."

"That's great! But how did she find them?"

"At his main office. She dropped by there one afternoon, when she knew Ron would be shacking with his lady friend. (Phil gave her the word on that.) And she went through all his monthly bank statements for the past year, which she found in one of his desk drawers. Then she took eighteen of the checks—some made out to a real estate company and the rest made out to a fancy boutique called Francine's. Well, after that it was fairly simple detective work. She got the chippy's address and quickly ascertained that the apartment building belonged to the real estate company named on the canceled checks. Then she called Francine's, pretending she wanted a credit reference on Carol Hall (that's the chippy's name), and they sweetly informed her that Miss Hall's monthly bills have always been promptly paid. So with that kind of ammunition she was ready to let him have it with both barrels."

"I should think she would!"

"But because of the financial jam he's in, she still doesn't want to leave him. She's particularly concerned about the house, which she doesn't want to lose because it's so perfect for the five kids she's got. And she's also ambivalent about Ron. In spite of his obvious whoring around. Just yesterday, while we were having this long martini lunch, she said, 'I really hate that crummy bastard, but I've got to admit he's awfully good in bed. Even with all his damned money problems, he's still like a bull in heat.' Those were her exact words: 'Like a bull in heat.' What's more, dear sisters, they've been loving like rabbits during all the time they've been arguing."

"You're kidding. You've got to be kidding, Selma," said Ruth, total disbelief in her prim, soft voice.

"I'm just as puzzled as you are, sweetie, but that's what Jan told me. In fact, she quite frankly says that their sex is always a lot more passionate after they've been fighting. And she further admitted that she will occasionally bitch at him and deliberately pick an argument in order to—"

"But that's vulgar!" exclaimed Ruth. "I can't believe she'd do such a thing."

"I not only believe it," said Graciela. "I sort of envy her. And you can call it anything you want, Ruth—it's still beautiful. Beautiful in a very basic sense. Because there's real passion there. And that's what we've lost, most of us, especially in our kind of so-called intellectual circles. We can act liberated, we can smoke pot like the kids, and we can even say 'shit' and 'fuck,' in mixed company, yet we can't have the kind of sex some of the squares have. Like Ron, for example. He'd never say 'fuck' in mixed company, and he won't let Jan say it either. But they sure know how to do it. While the rest of us *talk* instead of act. I think we've finally talked all the passion out of our lives."

"But some of us are squares both ways," said Ruth. "Look at us—at Walter and me. We never say it, and we never do it. We're uptight in all directions. And that's why I overreacted to Jan having sex that way. It just seemed . . . well . . . I can't really say."

"I've also overreacted," said Graciela with a wistful sigh. "I'm not really that taken by Jan's bull fever, although Ron's sexual prowess does have a certain appeal, especially when you compare him with a cold robot like Raul. But I'm not sure I could tolerate all that other *macho* crap he's been forcing on Jan. . . . And why should she agree to quit our group—now that she's got the upper hand? He's in a damned poor position to demand anything."

"Because he feels threatened by our consciousness raising," answered Selma. "Ever since our very first meeting, she's been a lot different at home. He hasn't been able to order her around like a stupid servant. Like getting her out of bed after midnight to fix a damned meal for his bowling buddies."

"He's actually done that?"

"Lots of times. He's done it for years. But not anymore—not since she's been with us. And that's why I begged her to stay on. Because she needs our kind of reinforcement, our support."

"Perhaps not," said Rachel. "She's already cut through his *machismo*. She's become a different woman, and he won't be able to change her back to that old submissive nice-mama role. At least I hope he won't."

"Then why would she accept his darned ultimatum about quitting us or quitting him?"

"Because she's gotten a few other concessions from him—aside from his promise to give up gambling and also his mistress. For example, she's going to have her

208

own bank account, with a monthly deposit that should easily cover all household bills and her own personal expenses. What's more, that money will come directly from the monthly receipts of the bowling alleys, and she's got the right to review all bank statements and company accountings, so that he can't write checks for any future mistress."

"That sounds like a palace revolt."

"It certainly is. And Jan has done most of this on her own, with only an occasional hint from her husband's cousin."

"But what's in it for Phil? Why should he get involved?"

"Well, first of all, he's always had a crush on Jan. Since high school. And, second, he hates Ron's guts. They were supposed to be partners when the first bowling alley was built, but Ron apparently screwed him out of the deal."

"And hell hath no fury like a partner scorned," said Rachel as if she'd been waiting for the cue. "So she couldn't hope for a more reliable ally."

"Are you saying that his hate is a better guarantee than his love?"

"I didn't mean it exactly that way. But that's pretty close to what I feel."

"Oh, that's terribly cynical, Rachel," exclaimed Ruth. "If it's mostly hate that motivates him, I'd rather go it alone if I were Jan. And I say that in spite of the awful loneliness I've felt these past few days—since I moved away from Walter."

"My gosh, Ruth! You certainly don't waste time. When did you move out?"

"Last Friday morning. As soon as Walter left for work, I packed my clothes and a few books and moved into a furnished apartment. And that's when the loneliness began. Not right away, of course, because I was too busy unpacking and settling in. But toward the end of the day, when it started getting dark, I suddenly felt like a lost orphan. So I turned on every light in the apartment and started cooking myself a cheese omelet, playing my kitchen radio much louder than usual and switching from one station to another. Then just as the cheese was beginning to melt, I turned off the stove and went out to eat at the most crowded restaurant I could find. And I stayed there longer than I should, slowly sipping three cups of coffee after dinner and self-consciously looking around to see if there was anyone I knew, hoping I wouldn't, because they might wonder why I was eating alone on a Friday night. So I immediately paid my bill and hurried away, driving back to the apartment in a roundabout way because I had automatically started back on the customary route to our house. I'd gone halfway before I realized my mistake. And when I finally got to my new place I was surprised to find all the lights still on, momentarily forgetting that I'd left them on. Anyway, as I looked around the living room, at the dull blank walls on every side, I suddenly remembered all the paintings we'd bought in France and Italy and the Etruscan vase Walter had given me on our fifth anniversary. We'll have to fight about them, I said to myself, because he likes them as much as I do.

"So thinking about the arguments I'd make to keep at least half of them, 1 walked into the kitchen to make myself some coffee. Then, as I turned on the front burner, I noticed the half-cooked omelet I'd left in the skillet. Well, that really got me. I mean the way that poor omelet looked. Now, I know this will sound crazy and all that—but it looked so shriveled up and so abandoned that it gave me this awful feeling. Because it looked the way I felt—completely abandoned and sort of useless. I knew that I was starting a new life, but I didn't feel very new. In fact, I felt suddenly older and little scared.

210

And—let's face it—I was feeling too damned sorry for myself. So I took my pot of Sanka to the bedroom and switched on my miniature TV set, catching the last half of a Bette Davis movie that made me feel so sorry for her that I temporarily forgot how sorry I was for myself. I've never seen such a gallant victim. . . ."

"She's really a winning loser," interjected Rachel. "My aunt called her 'the winningest loser in Hollywood.' But I'm beginning to suspect that all those Bette Davis and Joan Crawford movies—in fact, all the soap operas —are really part of a *macho* strategy to make women love their own suffering. The female stars generally win by losing, but your John Waynes and Gregory Pecks can only win by actually winning."

"Hey, sweetie! That's a darned interesting observation."

"But not particularly original, Selma, I must have read it somewhere. Maybe in *Ms.*"

"Wherever you got it, I think it's a really important aspect of the *macho* syndrome. And it makes me kind of sorry for all the poor men who think they've got to be total winners—like all the heroes in movies or TV shows. From the moment they can understand a complete sentence, males are being told they've got to win. And the pressure never lets up. Because no matter how much they manage to win now and then, there's always a bigger winner somewhere. . . . Maybe that's the reason men don't like movies as much as women do. We're merely comparing our sorrows with Bette Davis, while our men are competing with Steve McQueen."

"That's true most of the time," said Trudy. "But how about a movie like *Days of Wine and Roses*, where Jack Lemmon was an alcoholic?"

"Walter walked out on that one," said Ruth. "He hates downbeat pictures."

211

"So did my husband," added Selma. "And I'll bet that movie was never a box-office success."

"It had a copout ending," observed Trudy as an afterthought. "He seemed to be getting well at the end. They made you think he'd be okay. But that seldom happens. Certainly not with the alcoholics I've known."

"Okay now—we've gotten off the track again," said Selma. "We haven't heard the end of what Ruth was telling us."

Slightly more hesitant than before, Ruth asked someone where she'd left off, then continued in a voice that was barely audible.

"Well, after the Bette Davis movie I switched to the Dick Cavett show, but I really can't remember who he was interviewing because my mind was way off somewhere else. That often happens to me when I watch one of the talk shows. I'm generally alone in the guest room, because Walter's always asleep before they come on. So I find myself mumbling comments on what someone is saying, particularly if it's controversial, and I keep thinking about it way after that particular guest has been replaced by the next one. But on this particular night my interior thoughts had no relation to Dick Cavett's guests. I was mostly worrying about myself, wondering if I could really live alone, if I could actually teach again, if marriage is really a viable institution, if I could stand being old and living alone in that Menopause Manor in Mexico City, if, if, if, on and on, until I could barely keep my eyes open. But when I turned off the set and snuggled under the blankets, I couldn't fall asleep. So, after tossing around for an hour or so, I took a couple of pills from one of the bottles I had taken from Walter's side of the bathroom cabinet. He's always had ten or fifteen different kinds of pills—uppers, downers, sidewaysers, all kinds!"

"But why would a doctor take so many pills?" someone asked.

"Most doctors do," answered Ruth. "And I've often worried about Walter becoming addicted to the darned things."

"It's really an occupational hazard," said Selma. "As a matter of fact, I've got an article in this drawer that has some pretty scary statistics on what Ruth is talking about. Just listen to this:

> In a recent report to the membership, officials of the American Medical Association have declared that emotional problems, as well as drug addiction and alcoholism, almost amount to occupational hazards in the medical profession. They cite surveys indicating that nearly two percent of the doctors practicing in Oregon and Arizona have been disciplined by state authorities for drug abuse, and that an even larger number have been involved in excessive drinking.
>
> The report also refers to a 1964 study estimating that narcotics addiction among doctors is 30 to 100 times more common than in the general population. . . .

"My God, Selma!" someone exclaimed. "I really can't believe that. That's incredible."

"There's more, Trudy. Listen to this:

> . . . Suicides are also frequent among doctors. According to obituaries in the *Journal of the AMA* (which are generally quite specific about the exact cause of death), more than 250 doctors committed suicide in the 30-month period between May 1965 and November 1967. That number exceeds the combined total of deaths among doctors due to plane and auto accidents, drowning and homicide; and drug addiction or alcoholism were important factors in 40 percent of those suicides.

213

"Then, farther on, the article says there's been a conspiracy of silence among doctors to protect themselves from public exposure, but the truth has been leaking out anyway."

"It's certainly an open secret among the doctors I've known—especially the surgeons," said Ruth. "And I guess a lot of their wives fall into the same trap, because the damned pills are always around."

"You don't have to be a doctor's wife to make that scene," said Rachel. "I've been poppin' pills for a long time. Ever since I first got into the acting gig in one of those Off Broadway companies. Most of us were messing with pot, pills, and some of the hard stuff. I finally cut down on most of that stuff, but my husband's still heavy on greenies, pinkies, and hash. Like a lot of other actors I know, they seem to need them to get their juices going for each performance. At least that's what Jerry keeps telling himself. But I didn't realize surgeons had to pop a few uppers to get themselves ready to cut you open. Though it's certainly logical when you give it a second think. I sure wouldn't want to look at somebody's bloody insides without taking some kind of drug."

"Neither would I," said Isabel. "But sometimes I need a couple of pills just to face another empty day. Especially during these past few years, when everything seems to be slipping away. I get this awful sense of wasted years—day after day and month after month going down the drain. That's why I've decided to go back to college, even though I'm past forty. I've got to find something to fill that terrible void. There ought to be something more than dirty dishes and dirty kids. There has to be. . . ."

Once again there was a dead silence, as on other occasions when someone had touched on a problem that affected everyone. It was Graciela who finally spoke up.

"That's why I got into politics and the peace movement—to fill that void Isabel just mentioned. So it

214

wasn't idealism at first; it was just something to do, something that would take me out of my damned house, that I could also justify on more or less altruistic grounds. But after I got involved, I became genuinely idealistic. Perhaps too idealistic. And that's when I realized how sexist politics can be. All those so-called democrats doing their *macho* thing, conniving and pushing and double-crossing each other in that continuous struggle for status, and all us stupid females licking their envelopes and running for coffee and taking notes at their damned meetings and then getting the royal shaft when we ask for a little of that equality they're always harping about. And some of the worst *machos* are the biggest bleeders for all the poor minorities. They'll carry on like Jesus Christ about how the Southerners mistreat the blacks, pausing now and then to bitch like hell to an obviously over-worked waitress about a slightly overcooked steak that's being paid for by a campaign committee that is flat broke. Then boasting that he won't leave her a tip. And let me tell you something else: I once had dinner with a Republican candidate for state senator, with whom I had appeared on a local radio show. We had discussed busing, and he had presented the conservative view. But I've never seen any man treat a waitress with such courtesy, and it was an easy, natural kind of decency. Nothing forced or condescending. And knowing what a sexist bastard his opponent was, I almost voted for that Republican."

"You should have," said Rachel.

"Of course, you should," echoed Trudy.

"Well—to tell you the truth—that's exactly what I did. But Selma knows the Democrat who ran against him, and I hope she'll keep my secret."

"Of course I will," said Selma. "I didn't vote for him either. For the same reason. He's the lousiest sexist I've ever met. So I wrote in my own name. And so did my

215

husband. Then we looked through the newspapers to see if they'd reported my two votes on the official tally; but those damned *meshuggeners* completely ignored me. . . . But getting back to your comments about the way women get shafted by alleged idealists, I'm particularly reminded of the shafting we got at the Democratic Convention in Miami. We got all kinds of promises in the primaries: abortions on request, equal representation, equal voting power, equal this, and equal that. Then as soon as things got a little heavy for McGovern, all those promises began to fade. First of all came that crucial contest for equal female representation on the South Carolina delegation, and McGovern pledged his support to the Women's Caucus. But suddenly his key operators were all over the convention floor ordering the troops to vote against the women *because George needs it that way.* Then a few hours later the same staff people told everyone to vote against the minority report on abortion, and I saw Bella Abzug and Gloria Steinem really telling those bastards off. But somehow McGovern persuaded good old Shirley MacLaine to sell her sweet soul, and she got up and made that speech she didn't believe in. She even told a TV reporter that she agreed with her sisters, but that the abortion issue would embarrass George in the campaign. . . ."

"Incidentally," said Rachel, breaking through Selma's increasingly bitter recapitulation. "I have a friend who was one of McGovern's female patsies on the California delegation, and she told me about a conversation she overheard in one of the hotel lobbies, where Bella and Gloria cornered Shirley and gave her such a bawling out that Shirley was actually in tears, begging them to understand why she had double-crossed them. But they still never forgave her."

"And why should they?" asked Selma. "She helped the McGovern people as they ganged up against Sissy

Farenthold when she ran against Eagleton for the Vice Presidential nomination. I understand Sissy had more than a hundred votes in the California delegation, but Shirley helped the McGovern *machos* to pass on the first roll call so that they could twist a few female arms to reduce that vote for Sissy. Once again because it might embarrass poor old George. And everyone knew damned well poor old George was personally directing all those votes against the women, although he tried to give the impression that his managers were acting on their own—that he was still as pure as the South Dakota snow.

"Well, after all that crap in Miami I decided to give myself a vacation from politics. Especially after I read an interview of Gary Hart, where he told a reporter that there weren't any women at the higher echelon of McGovern's staff because there weren't any females who were skilled or experienced enough to hold such positions. So I said to hell with all those sexist *nudniks*. I wouldn't have licked a single envelope or rung a single doorbell for that kind of crowd. And if I didn't have such a deep antagonism to Nixon, I wouldn't have voted for McGovern."

"That's how I felt," said Graciela. "They sure didn't get any help from me. Not after Miami. I sat out that election."

"Well, I still voted Democratic," said Trudy reluctantly. "But I didn't lick a single envelope."

There were several more expressions of disenchantment with McGovern, mostly relating to his staff's conduct at the convention and with what they characterized as McGovern's shillyshallying on the campaign promises. There were also a few disparaging comments on what someone called "that *macho* charade by his three campaign chairmen," each of whom tried to hog the headlines, no matter how much their status struggle might harm the candidate. And all six women agreed that Sissy Farenthold would have been the best choice for the Vice Presidential nomination. Then, as they were having a coffee break, Ruth told someone she would have to leave earlier than usual.

"I'd like to get back to the apartment before the garage attendant leaves," she said. "I know it sounds silly, but I'm frankly a little scared of walking through that dark underground corridor, especially after midnight. I guess I'm overreacting to all those news reports about women getting raped, but I really can't help myself."

"Listen, Ruthie, there's no reason to apologize," said Selma. "I'm also worried about rapists—most of us are—but I'm especially worried about Shari being attacked. She's always hitchhiking to the beach, sometimes alone. Like all these teen-agers do. I keep showing her newspaper clippings about girl hitchhikers being raped and murdered, and she simply laughs at me. As if it could never happen to her."

"That's exactly what Erlinda does," said Graciela, referring to her teen-age daughter. "Raul and I are always warning her, but she just shrugs her shoulders and keeps on hitchhiking. I keep hoping she'll get arrested someday, which might scare her a little."

"Or merely antagonize her."

"Maybe so, Rachel. She's already a bit of a cop hater because of the Salazar case."

"Perhaps your daughters should talk to my niece," suggested Isabel. "She was raped a couple of years ago. Just outside of Boston. She was picked up on a highway by a forty-year-old man who looked like a typical suburban husband—well dressed, apparently well educated, and seemingly harmless. But when they got to a lonely stretch of road, he suddenly turned off into a deserted picnic area, telling Nancy that he had to check one of his rear tires because he felt a pull to one side.

218

Then, after going through that pretense, he got back in the car and started to make a pass at her. She kidded him at first, letting him know that he was old enough to be her father, then quickly realized he was dead serious. But when she tried to get out, he pulled her back, yanked off her jeans, and soon overpowered her because she was afraid he'd kill her. She had remembered someone saying that when a woman's facing a madman, it's safer to yield. So she reluctantly stopped struggling and let him go ahead, crying all the while and inwardly vowing to have her revenge. And when he finally let her out of the car at the first intersection they came to, she took down his license number, then ran to a gas station to call her mother. Fortunately for that filthy rapist, her father is dead. I think Arthur would have killed him or would have tried to. . . ."

"Then what happened?"

"Well, as soon as they got home, her mother (that's my sister Fran) called the police and reported the whole thing. And that was the beginning of a miserable farce, though I guess farce is the wrong word, because there was nothing at all funny about it. In fact, it was pretty damned grim. . . . The officer who took the call seemed rather indifferent, but he finally told Fran that he'd send someone to their house to get a full report. Well, three hours later a couple of uniformed policemen showed up in a squad car, and right away they started cross-examining my niece as if *she* were the rapist instead of the victim, smiling at each other as she told them what happened and interrupting her with badgering questions. 'Why didn't you scream for help? Why didn't you keep struggling? Did you scratch his face or pull his hair?' And when Nancy told them she'd been afraid to resist because he might kill her, one of the cops said, 'So you decided to lay back and enjoy it—right?' Which, of course, angered the hell out of my sister, but he merely smiled and said,

219

'That was only a joke, lady. Don't take it so personal.' "
"That's awful!" someone exclaimed. "She should have reported him."

"Well, it got a lot worse," said Isabel. "When they went to the district attorney's office a few days later, they were told it would be difficult to prove the charge—that the accused man had denied raping Nancy. That he had told them it was *she* who had made the first advances and had even told him where to park the car. So it was her word against his. Then, as the real clincher, the DA told Fran and Nancy that you can't prove rape in a criminal trial without a corroborating eyewitness. So he dropped the case—refused to act."

"But that's absurd!" exclaimed Ruth. "Who would ever rape a woman in front of a witness?"

"You'd have to have a gang rape, with one man squealing on the others," said Rachel. "And that's not likely to happen."

"Anyway," said Isabel with bitter resentment in every word, "that's the law. He showed it to my sister in black and white. And that's why thousands of rapists go free to go on raping anyone they please."

"I've had big arguments with my husband about that stupid law," said Trudy. "And he's always given me the typical lawyer's response: You've got to protect innocent men who might be accused by a vengeful woman. He keeps saying that most rapes are nothing more than ambivalent fornication—that most women want a little force in order to overcome their chastity compulsion—and then he closes his argument with that old defense lawyer's proverb that 'you can't thread a moving needle.' Which simply means that a woman's got to resist until she's killed by some maniac."

"That's a lot of *macho* crap," Selma snapped. "Especially those catchy phrases about ambivalent fornication and chastity compulsion. Some men assume that we are all dying to get laid by just anyone, that we can't distinguish between a rapist and a lover. But all that talk is simply a justification for violence."

"I'm not so sure," said Trudy, drawing out the phrase as if to assess each word separately. "I'll agree that many cases are actual rape. But sometimes there *is* an element of real ambivalence. It's happened to me. I've had at least four or five affairs in the past few years, where each one began with some pretty coercive seduction. I'd allow myself to get into some preliminary necking, telling myself it was just harmless flirtation; then I'd start resisting when things got hot, struggling and angrily protesting, but still wanting him. And when he'd finally succeed, I'd be all his. What's more, I've often been a little disdainful when a man gives up too easily, when he thinks *no* always means *no*. And maybe that's what happens with some female hitchhikers. Certain men just assume that those girls are actually (or subconsciously) looking for sex, that they know all about the danger of seduction or rape, but are still willing to risk it. And in some cases the men may be right in making that assumption. So, as much as I disagree with my husband about a lot of things, I can't entirely dismiss his theory on ambivalent fornication. Not when I consider my own experiences."

"That's also happened to me," said Graciela. "I particularly remember a rather passionate scene with one of my favorite professors. We started necking on the couch in his office, but when he suddenly got serious, I started struggling like a scared virgin—which I wasn't— but he finally did what I really wanted him to do. Then he got worried and begged me not to tell anyone that he had forced me. 'I merely wanted to seduce you.' Those were his exact words. I remember writing them down in my diary that night. . . . Yet, in spite of what we've just admitted, Trudy, I still think there's a big difference

221

between rape and ambivalent fornication. And I'm totally opposed to any law that says you can't convict a man of rape unless there's an eyewitness to corroborate the woman's complaint. That's a vicious law that all women should try to repeal. Like they've done to some of those stupid abortion laws."

"There's already a movement against them," observed Selma. "I've gotten some literature from NOW and one or two other Women's Lib groups, and I've sent them my check for the political and legal campaigns they've started in several states."

"Give me their addresses after the meeting," said Trudy. "And I'll send them a few bucks."

"So will I," said four or five voices crisscrossing each other.

"But we've also got to get involved more directly," said Selma. "There will be petitions to sign and circulate among our friends and maybe some marches to the state legislature and the governor's office."

"Well, I'm not much of a marcher anymore," said Ruth. "All those peace marches I've gotten into the last two years sort of drained me. When I was mingling with all those thousands of wonderful people, I had the illusion of real progress—that peace had to come—but then came the bombing of Haiphong, and it all seemed utterly pointless and kind of naïve. But there was something else about those marches that disturbed me. They were always dominated by men who seemed terribly ego-involved and sort of conniving. Worse than that, they were all kind of sexist. They expected women to do all the cruddy menial stuff, while they pushed each other for the spotlight. Just look at the roster of speakers for any of those meetings, and you'll find nothing but males. Except for Coretta King, because she was black— and, even so, they always introduced her as Mrs. Martin Luther King."

"But you've also had Jane Fonda."

"Yes, but she's been holding her own peace rallies and, incidentally, doing a damned good job."

"I'm beginning to see your point, Ruth. I hadn't really considered the male-female aspect of the peace movement, but now that you mention it, I guess you're right. The women do the marching and the men do the speechmaking."

"How true that is." Rachel sighed. "And I'm just now remembering what that great liberal Dr. Spock said about women on a television show. . . ."

"What did he say?"

"That a woman's main function is being a good mother and keeping a nice home."

"You're kidding! Not Dr. Spock!"

"I wish to heaven I were kidding, Trudy. But I heard him say it with my own ears. And he was dead serious."

"That's the tragic thing about so many supposedly liberal men," said Graciela. "They have a blind spot when it comes to women. They can easily see all the prejudice that's directed against blacks, Chicanos, and any other oppressed group, but they can be totally oblivious to any crap that's directed against us women. In fact, much of the crap comes from them."

"But sometimes they can't help it," said Selma. "We'll have to admit that they're also victims of the same *macho* values that affect everyone. Take my husband, for example. He's as liberal about women as any man I know. He's the one who literally forced me to march in that big Women's Lib demonstration, and he marched with me—holding a poster he had made himself. And around our house, he's always trying to play down this business of sex roles, telling the kids that there's no such thing as female chores and male chores, doing a lot of kitchen work himself to set an example for the boys. But,

223

like I've said before, he's got a lot of old sexist hangups (subtle, unconscious ones) that occasionally crop up. And no matter how much I might bitch about them, I later realized—reluctantly, of course—that he was raised by a Portnoy's mother. And when you've been spoiled by that kind of mama, you're almost bound to be a *macho*.

"And look at me. Mrs. Portnoy's daughter. Getting ten lessons a day on how to marry a doctor and another ten lessons on how to castrate him. And after that, a few more lessons on how to raise your sons so that they won't be castrated by another Mrs. Portnoy's daughter. And while I was learning all those lessons and counterlessons, I was also learning how to make the best chicken soup you've ever tasted."

"But Mama Portnoy isn't the only offender," said Graciela. "You should see how Mama Gomez raises her sons, her *machos*. And just remember, Selma, that *machismo* is a Spanish word. And among Mexicans or Chicanos, that's not considered a derogatory term. Our men are proud of their *machismo*, they want to be called *machos*. What's more, most of their mothers want them to be *muy macho, muy hombre*. And most of them also expect and tolerate a lot of sexist crap from their husbands because they themselves have been taught to. My mother, for example, used to wait on my dad as if he were a boss instead of a husband. And he never in his life cooked anything or washed a single dish. That would have been an insult to his damned *machismo*, and I say this in spite of the fact that I literally worshiped him. But he was no different from any other man in our *barrio*. And like them, he also fooled around with other women and occasionally came home with lipstick on his shirt and their cheap perfume reeking from his body."

"What would your mother do?"

"Nothing really. She might grumble a little, but she'd let it pass. She'd been taught by her mother that men are different from their wives—that they need other women to satisfy their enormous sexual needs. She'd also been taught that sex was dirty, that decent women—*mujeres decentes*—had sex only to bear children. Never for pleasure. Only whores did it for pleasure. And she started to sell me the same crap when I got to be a teen-ager. She thought it was perfectly okay (in fact, very desirable) for my brothers to chase after any chippy they could find, to test their *machismo*—but I was supposed to remain a virgin until I was lucky enough to get married. That was my mother's main goal: to get me married. My desire to be a teacher was accepted as a mere stopgap, and because teaching was also *una profesión decente* and therefore okay for a woman. Pity me if I dared to become an actress or an airline stewardess. She would have sent me to see a priest. So the point I'm getting at—and it's the same as Selma's—is that women are probably as much to blame for *machismo* as men are. We've got an awful lot to undo just within ourselves."

"We've also got to adjourn," said Selma. "It's already half past twelve."

XII

Runaway Children—
Stay-around Spouses

> *Thus the psychological portrait of the individual and powerless woman consists of naïveté, compulsive heterosexuality, procreative "pride," fearfulness, self-hatred, mistrust of other women—and of compassion, passion and idealism.*
>
> —Phyllis Chesler,
> *Women and Madness*

AS the meeting was about to begin, Selma received a phone call that temporarily delayed their discussion, but she rejoined the group less than a minute later.

"That was my husband calling," she said, a weary anxiety in her usually salty manner. "From Taos, New Mexico. He's been looking for Jerry, our oldest son, but hasn't found him yet."

"That's a long way from here."

"It sure is, Rachel. And not too easy to reach by air. Alvin had to switch planes three times."

"How would Jerry get there?"

"Hitchhiking, I guess. His roommate at Berkeley told us that he'd suddenly disappeared about a week ago, probably stoned out of his mind. He'd mentioned Taos several times, so his friends figure that's where he most likely went. But he could have gone to Boulder or Cambridge, where Alvin found him the last time he took off."

"Couldn't the police help you locate him?"

"Not unless he's been arrested. Otherwise, they can't be bothered. There are just too damned many teen-agers floating around, drifting from one pad to another, restlessly searching for God knows what and never giving a damn how much worry they're causing at home. Worry, worry, worry—that's all we've done these past few years. I keep wishing there were some way to turn it off, to forget all about them for a while. Just long enough to give me a bit more perspective on this mother thing. So that I might somehow learn how to love them again—not because I *have* to love them but because I really do. Which doesn't make much sense, but that's how. . . ."

"Makes sense to me," said Rachel. "Because that's exactly how I feel about my kids. But I keep wondering if I'll ever be able to love them again. I mean the way I'm supposed to."

"Of course you will!" exclaimed Ruth. "They're your own flesh and blood. You've got to."

"That's what they keep telling us." Selma sighed. "You've got to love your kiddies. But, like Rachel, I also wonder if it's really possible after you've gone through all that day-to-day hassle, the arguing and bitching, the threats and counterthreats, the screaming and crying, the grudging apologies and petulant silences, and all that mother guilt that keeps gnawing at you and making you resent them all the more because you can't stand the guilt. So—considering all that—I'd have to say that I'm probably happier with my husband than I am with my kids, particularly since they've become teen-agers. And Alvin often says the same thing. In fact, most of the major arguments between us—most of the tensions in our household—arise from some problem we're having with Shari, Jerry, or Sid. We'll disagree on how we should deal with one or the other, and suddenly we're having a real brawl. That's why we're both so anxious to have them grow up and get out on their own."

"But aren't there days," asked Ruth, "when you actually enjoy having them with you?"

"Damned few, to be perfectly honest. Maybe ten or fifteen percent of the time."

"If you're lucky," added Graciela.

"That's right, Grace. You've got to be lucky. But most of the time they're likely to be headaches. Problems with schoolwork. Problems with drugs or drinking. Problems with boyfriends or girlfriends. Sudden pregnancies and emergency abortions—though I'm still knocking on wood as far as Shari's concerned. Then there's always that boredom they keep griping about as they sulk around the house, slopping up their bedrooms, messing the kitchen, and playing that loud crappy music that pounds through the walls every damned night and all day and night on weekends. And there's that nasty vulgar language they use. If I had talked to my parents the way they talk to me, I would have had my face bashed in. But I guess we're mostly to blame for that—Alvin and I. We thought it was cute and liberated to let them talk that way, that it was hypocritical to forbid them to use some of the vulgar language we use. But I'm beginning to realize how ugly it is in teen-agers, especially girls. . . ."

"Wait a minute," Trudy interjected. "I may agree with you about teen-agers cussing, but why is it worse for girls?"

"Because it is," said Selma. "I know that's discriminating, and I'm a hypocrite for thinking that way, but that's how I honestly feel. Even though I've got a pretty foul tongue myself. Which, incidentally, I've been trying to curb lately, as you may have noticed, or at least I hope you have. Somebody—perhaps it was someone in this group—recently told me that I talk like Dita Beard, and that sort of floored me. Who wants to talk like her? Anyway, I started cussing like a man when I was a freshman—I mean freshwoman or freshperson or fresh whatever—in college. Just for the shock value, and because it got me a few laughs. Which is one of my compulsions, I guess—to get laughed at. . . ."

"Laughed *with*," said Rachel.

"That's a kind way to put it, sweetie, but I'm afraid it's mostly laughed *at*, especially when you're no longer young and pretty. Like a lot of other things, cursing is a lot less attractive in older women."

"Now you're being a sexist," protested Trudy. "You're making language a—"

"Okay, I'm a sexist," said Selma, interrupting her. "When it comes to cussing, I'm a sexist—even though I've got the foulest tongue in this group. That's one prerogative the males can have, and I'm sorry I ever horned in on them. Particularly when I hear Shari following in my footsteps, using the word 'shit' as if it were a comma—not even an exclamation point, mind you! What used to be cute and liberated seems stupid and vulgar when you give it a hard second look."

"You're overreacting," mumbled Trudy.

"Maybe I am, Trudy. This business of Jerry suddenly disappearing again has gotten me down. Really down. I've been reassessing our attitudes all the way down the line, and no one in our family comes out very well. It's such a damned mess, and I'm so terribly guilt-ridden. But mostly I'm so tired, tired, tired of worrying about my kids and arguing with Alvin about what we should do about them. All things considered, I'd

229

rather divorce my children than my husband. Without them around, he'd be a cinch to live with. So would I. I'm sure of that."

"That's exactly how I feel," said Graciela. "If anything would keep me from divorcing Raul, it's the horrible prospect of being left alone with my two teen-agers. I know that's a horrible thing to say, but I might as well be frank about it. They're the ones I'd really like to divorce. . . . Nevertheless, I keep blaming myself (and Raul) for the way we've raised them. Maybe I'm mostly responsible for what they've become—allowing them too damned much freedom when they were young, spoiling them out of guilt. Who the hell knows? I'm so tired of thinking about it."

"That's the rub, all right," said Selma, sighing sadly between phrases. "That's the real rub, Gracie. That load of guilt you carry around. I kept telling myself not to press them too hard, to relax, to give them enough room to develop into real human beings. I even went easy on the sex and pot business because I didn't want to be a middle-class square, and Alvin went along with me. Then, suddenly it all went sour on us. Jerry got whacked on LSD and bennies and dropped out of school because he thought it was 'like a drag, man'—whatever the hell that means. Shari went from pot to hash and started missing school because she's always oversleeping and doesn't do her homework. And now we're told that most of the kiddies at Sid's junior high school are popping pills and blowing pot. So almost every night, Alvin and I sit around wondering where the hell we went wrong. What should we have done differently that wouldn't have caused a whole new set of problems at the other extreme?"

"What other extreme?" asked Ruth.

"Like having dull uptight kids with proper clothes

and crew cuts and Nixon-Agnew posters in their bedrooms."

"Gee, Selma, I think I'd almost settle for that. At
least they wouldn't worry you sick. I could use a little
bourgeois dullness at our house. It would be kind of nice
to have a daughter who would call me mother instead of
nosy old bitch. But as I'm saying all this—obviously
referring to Erlinda and her special brand of teen-age
bitchiness—I keep remembering how bitchy I was with
my own mother, how I used to sulk around the house,
messing up the kitchen and allowing my bedroom to
become a pigsty before I'd finally clean up—always
under pressure. No wonder my parents just smile when I
complain to them about Erlinda. But is that supposed to
be our final triumph—to be able to give *our* kids that
same smug smile when they start complaining about *their*
teen-agers? Because if that's all the satisfaction there is,
why should anyone bother? I don't want that kind of
delayed revenge. It's so damned repetitive and cyclical.
And ultimately futile. Generation after generation going
through the same damned cycle of errors and misery—
daughter like mother like daughter. . . ."

"And son like father like son," Trudy added.

"That, too, of course. But I don't seem to relate to
my son in the same way. For example, I keep seeing
myself in both my daughter and my mother, but I seldom
see myself in my son or my father. The connections are
somehow different. Consequently, I can't love them or
hate them in the same way. There's a certain physical
and psychic distance between me and the males in my
family—between me and my son and my husband and
my father—that I can't put into words. Which might be
true of all males and females. Or does that make sense to
any of you?"

"It does to me," said Rachel. "I've always felt that

231

difference in my relations with Jean and Benjie, and I think it's mostly biological."

"How so?"

"Well, let me put it this way, Ruth. My daughter and I (like all females) both know the misery of menstruation, and we're also blessed or cursed with the same vaginal systems, the same breast apparatus. And, perhaps just as important, we've been assigned the same kind of female roles from the day we were born, with the same rages and frustrations that all of us are bound to experience. Consequently, we have what my doctor calls a symbiotic relationship which men don't have."

"Then why don't mothers and daughters get along better?"

"I frankly don't know, Trudy. But maybe it's because we can't fool each other as easily as we can fool our menfolks. We're all kind of mysterious to men. They simply don't know what's happening to us—physically or psychologically—when we get our menstrual headaches, our stomach cramps, our nausea, our sudden moodiness; but they do worry about us and probably have an exaggerated notion of what's going on. They're perpetually afraid that we're liable to crack up at any time, so when they see our tears and our lips trembling, they generally let us have our way. That's why I call it the tyranny of tears. Which most of us practice."

"But that's a terrible accusation," protested Selma with a barely repressed chuckle. "I only cry when it's for real."

"And when nothing else works," Rachel added. "You're not kidding me, sweetie. In fact, it's pretty darned difficult for any of us females to fool one another with tears. My mother could always con my daddy and my brothers with a sudden headache or a mess of tears, but she knew that I knew it was all a put-on. And whenever I had the curse, daddy would hover around me as if I were on my deathbed, telling me I didn't have to wash dishes or go to school, and a few minutes later mama would be yanking me out of bed and ordering me to get moving—curse or no curse. So, as my grandmother used to say, you can always love those you can deceive, but you tend to dislike people who catch on to you."

"Oh, Rachel, you're such a cynic," said Ruth with affectionate envy in her voice. "You keep reminding me of my own little deceptions. And I guess that's one of the few satisfactions of being a female: We're all such experts at playing games. And we so often play them even when they aren't necessary—deceiving when there's no need to deceive—as if we're always practicing for what my husband calls the big game, that final crucial match that never. . . ."

"Now who's being the cynic?"

"I guess I am, Trudy. As a matter of fact, I've always had the feeling that I'm part of a vast female conspiracy that's forever plotting to survive against an overpowering enemy. It's a feeling I got from my mother, who (like so many Southern women) was always involved in this or that strategy or subterfuge, trying to get something or accomplish something by indirection be-cause she knew my father would refuse an outright request. But he himself seemed to enjoy her little games, probably because it made her seem more feminine. . . ."

"And because her need to be tricky was also an affirmation of his male power," said Rachel. "That's why almost any Southerner prefers a two-faced grinning Uncle Tom. He knows that Tom probably hates him as much as any black militant, but that Negro's ass-licking deceitfulness simply affirms his white man's sense of power. So—like most women—my black brothers and sisters have become real experts at deception. For survival, if nothing else."

"That reminds me of something Alvin mentioned

233

last winter," said Selma. "He'd been watching a football game between two black college teams, and he told me it was the trickiest game he'd ever seen—that both sides played like a bunch of magicians, like the Harlem Globetrotters on a football field."

"They certainly do," said Rachel. "And that's another facet of what I'm talking about. I'm beginning to think that our trickiness-for-survival has become just plain old trickiness-for-fun."

"An ethnic imperative," suggested Trudy. "We Jews know all about that."

"Hey now—you're getting heavy."

"I'm serious, Selma. I really think that all powerless groups develop certain habits of mind that are necessary for survival against those in power. Blacks, Jews, Chicanos, and women—we're all in the same boat in this respect. And like all the others, we females have developed a sort of guerrilla temperament, relying on deception and indirection or cleverness and guile—while our menfolk rely mostly on conventional power. Brute force."

"But they also have their bag of tricks," said Graciela.

"Full of holes."

"What's full of holes, Rachel?"

"Their bag of tricks, sweetie. And most of their tricks are pretty old and worn out. Power is their main weapon—money and power. They hardly need tricks."

"Then what would happen in a matriarchy?" asked Ruth. "What if *we* had the power?"

"Exactly the opposite: The males would start playing the same kind of games that we've been playing."

"You mean female games?"

"But they're not *female* games," said Trudy. "We don't play them because we're females; we play them because we're powerless, because there is sometimes no other way to move around or against the men in our lives—husbands, fathers, bosses, lovers, landlords, cops or whoever. And that's the worst part of being a female in a *macho* society—you've got to become devious and obsequious. Or at least we've been taught to think so, which is just as bad. And it's become so much a part of me—this damned trickiness we've been talking about—that I'm not sure I could play it straight anymore. I'm always wondering what role I should play in this or that situation and whether it's possible to deal with any man without worrying about his damned ego. Or maybe I'm just worrying about *my* ego and playing my little games because I don't want him to reject me. Because I want to be wanted—like all those TV models wearing this perfume or using that toothpaste, as if pleasing a man is the only reason for living. And it doesn't do any good to junk all that cosmetic crap, because I still want to be wanted. Not by my husband—not anymore—but by some kind of man I haven't met yet. Someone I won't have to play games with. Which brings me back to—to God knows where. I'm talking in circles again, going from nowhere to nowhere. But thanks for listening anyway. I'll sort out my thoughts some other time."

"Why wait?" said Selma. "Sort them out right now."

"They're just feelings, Selma. Muddled feelings. They haven't jelled into ideas yet."

"But your feelings are just as important as your ideas, Trudy. That's why we're here—to let it all out. Feelings and all."

"Especially our feelings," added Ruth.

"I know that. And I really appreciate it," said Trudy, a sudden huskiness in her usually crisp voice. "That's why I hate to quit coming. You've been so wonderful—all of you. These meetings are the best thing that ever happened. . . ."

"But why are you quitting?"

"Because I have to. I'm finally going back to work. Next Monday. On the job I mentioned a couple of weeks ago."

"Documentary films?"

"Right, Selma. I'll be working with an old friend of mine. And I'll have an awfully tough schedule—getting Ronnie ready for that special school and then rushing down to the studio. Then back home to fix our supper."

"Couldn't you get the same sitter you've had for Thursday nights?"

"That's not the problem, Graciela. It's having to get up at six A.M. and getting enough sleep to do a decent day's work. But maybe I can come back later on—when I've gotten more secure on this new job. I'm frankly a little scared right now. I've been out of filmmaking for an awful long time."

"Don't worry, Trudy. You'll make it."

"I'm not so sure. There've been a lotta changes these past few years. New cameras with special zoom lenses, new sound equipment, new editing apparatus—all kinds of new gadgets that I've got to learn about, even though I may not handle them myself."

"Then why must you learn?"

"Because I've got to know their scope and potential —time and cost factors—in order to budget each film. And with the tight shooting schedules I've seen, I'm sorta worried—I mean about really fitting in. Especially if I'm working with a bunch of men who might possibly resent taking orders from a female."

"Oh, God, here comes that *macho* crap again. Never fails."

"I've also got a reentry problem," said Graciela. "One of my old friends has promised me a job starting next month, but it's only provisional. I'll be assigned to a regular third-grade class for a while, but he wants me to

236

take some night courses in bilingual education, so that he can switch me to one of the *barrio* schools."

"Well, that should be a cinch for you."

"Not necessarily, Ruth. My Spanish is pretty rusty. Besides, I'll be teaching Puerto Rican kids, and their lingo is a bit different from my Chicana way of talking. And I don't know whether I'll be using conventional Spanish or a ghetto dialect. There's a big dispute about which language is most effective."

"That sounds like the argument my people have been having about using black English or regular English," observed Rachel.

"I guess so. But, quite frankly, it's all Greek to me—I mean this whole new concept of bilingual instruction. Some of the manuals I've been reading have got me completely befuddled. I keep running into phrases like 'differentiated levels of cognitive complexity' or something like 'phonemic distortions,' and they really floor me. I feel completely out of it."

"Perhaps no one else understands those terms—including the people who invented them."

"That's possible," said Graciela. "Anyway, I'll soon find out. I'll be starting one of those night courses next week. So that puts me in the same bag as Trudy: I've got to quit this nice group, and I really hate to leave. I don't think I would have moved out of my rut without our consciousness raising. I had almost resigned myself to perpetual housekeeping and total motherhood. So I've really got to thank all of you."

"My God, this sounds like a mass exodus," exclaimed Isabel. "I'm also pulling out. For a couple of months at least. Chris and I are going down to Mexico, for two months, and we're leaving the kids with my sister, thank God."

"That's a long vacation."

"Well, it's not exactly a vacation. At least, not for

Chris. He'll be giving a course in advanced surgery techniques at the university medical school. It's some kind of foundation deal that he got through a former classmate at Johns Hopkins. And I'll be going on some archaeological digs at Oaxaca, hoping it will be useful when I finally go back to college for a teacher's certificate."

"That sounds wonderful, Isabel."

"It certainly does. But I don't think I would have had the courage (or desire) to do such a wild thing if I hadn't come to these meetings. I would have felt too guilty about leaving my kids for two months. Just imagine how marvelous that will be! Eight whole weeks without them."

"You must have a wonderful sister."

"I sure do. You've all got to meet Liz some day. She's one of us. As a matter of fact, we've made a long-range deal. She'll take over my kids for two months every year, and I'll do the same for her."

"Does she have teen-agers?"

"Yes, they're the same ages as my kids, and they've always liked each other. So everyone's happy with the arrangement."

"Including your husbands?"

"I guess so. But it wouldn't make any difference whether they approve or disapprove. Liz and I are doing it for *our* convenience—not theirs."

"*Olé,* sister!" yelled Graciela. "That's the way we should all be thinking."

"I sure wish I had a sister like that," Rachel mused longingly. "But mine is so uptight I'm afraid my kids would be traumatized in less than a week. Either that, or they'd traumatize *her.* And there's no telling how her husband, Ernest, would take it. He's one of those hush-voiced undertakers who can't get used to real live people. You've got to act like a corpse or a bereaved

238

relative when Ernie's around; otherwise, he starts twitching and mumbling under his breath."

"What are their kids like?"

"They've only got one, and she's already a corpse. I've never seen a quieter child—quiet and strangely distant, as if her real self is somewhere else. And yet I occasionally see a sudden glint in her eye and a faint tremor on her lips, like she's about to explode. But when I mentioned this to Sis a few months ago, it didn't faze her one bit. 'Lucy's all right,' she said. 'She never bothers anyone. And she's perfect at school—straight A's in all her courses except one. That was a B minus in gym, which really upset her. She hates to disappoint her daddy.' And knowing Ernie, I'm sure he'd let her know."

"Would he really scold her?"

"No—I don't think he's capable of raising his voice. He'd merely sulk . . . and maybe twitch a little. So it would be a noiseless reprimand—exactly what you'd expect from an undertaker."

"But how can your sister put up with all that? It sounds kind of weird to me."

"Oh, she'd never complain. Sis worships that man, or at least she's in awe of him. And she's certainly proud of his financial success. So she's perfectly content to provide him with the quiet household he demands and a daughter who makes no fuss for anyone."

"How about rock music? Doesn't she ever play that kind of stuff? At least in her own room?"

"Not that I know of. She seems to prefer the classics. Mozart and Bach."

"Now that would be nice," said Isabel. "I'd give anything to have my kids play Bach instead of rock. That sure would be a welcome change. Heavenly."

"It would be heavenly all right," agreed Rachel. "But as I said before, that kind of household would drive my teen-agers up the damned wall. So I'll have to keep them at home. Even if I start working again, which doesn't seem likely."

"Why not?"

"Because there's a lot more competition than there used to be. There're hundreds of new black actors and actresses, and all of them are itching to do the kind of TV commercials and bit parts I used to do. Never mind the real acting roles. I'm out of that competition. So maybe I'll have to go back to college and learn something else. Like social work or baby-sitting."

"I'm facing the same problem," said Selma with a heavy sigh. "There's also a glut of talent in my field. There must be thousands of psychologists and psychiatrists with brand-new diplomas and nowhere to work. Yet there are damned few who are really capable of helping women patients."

"Why is that?"

"Well, first of all, about ninety percent of American psychiatrists and psychologists are male, and they have a patriarchal bias in their definitions of mental health. In other words, the norms for female behavior are determined by men, and they're consequently different from the norms for male behavior."

"You've lost me there, Selma. Could you make it more explicit?"

"I'll try, Isabel, but it's not entirely clear to me either. Anyway, let's say that women are classified as 'healthy,' 'neurotic,' or even 'psychotic' according to a male standard of mental health, which is based on a whole pattern of *macho* assumptions. And, as you might expect, the main assumption is that the 'normal' woman is an unemployed housewife."

"That figures," said Graciela. "That's certainly my husband's assumption."

"But it's also the standard of most professional psychiatrists and psychologists, including the ten percent who are female clinicians. This was brought out in a study by someone named Inge Broverman, who interviewed forty-six male and thirty-three female clinicians, most of whom feel that healthy women differ from healthy men because they're presumably more submissive, less independent, less adventurous, more easily influenced, less competitive, more delicate physically, more excitable in minor crises, more vain about personal appearance, less objective, less aggressive, and less capable in math and science. Consequently, their bias reflects the bias of the society as a whole. But here's the catch: When a woman fully acts out her assigned 'female' role, becoming timid, nonaggressive, passive, and submissive, she's liable to be classified as neurotic."

"So you can't win either way," observed Rachel. "Unless you reject that role from the very beginning."

"And that's not easy," said Selma. "Because women who reject the accepted female standards or become ambivalent about them sometimes frighten the people around them—or themselves—and they're frequently ostracized."

"Or they shut themselves off."

"That, too," agreed Selma. "And our high rate of depression, anxiety neuroses, psychosomatic illness, and suicide attempts are mostly due to that conditioned female behavior—that constant self-devaluation, eating one's anger and frustration, turning it all in, and eventually falling apart. Then seeking help because that's also part of our female conditioning. Men are supposed to see it through on their own and consequently get more ulcers and heart attacks. But women have therapy. In fact, most psychosurgery and electroshock treatment is performed on women. And there again, you get into that vicious cycle. Women seeking therapy are almost always treated by male doctors in a very patriarchal setting, thus being reexposed to the *macho* stand-

241

ards that led to her breakdown in the first place. Except that she's now treated as a *female child,* who is considered 'sick' or 'improving' in relation to her adjustment to what is supposedly healthy for females. In other words, she'll eventually be diagnosed as 'cured' if her therapist thinks she can now function—at least superficially—as wife and mother, no matter what kind of husband or children she has. Then she's permitted to go back to her 'normal' life until the next time she falls apart because of her basic inability to accept that narrowly defined role of the male's ideal female."

"But there must be some institutions or therapists who don't function according to that *macho* standard."

"Damned few—if any, Ruth. As a matter of fact, Otto Rank once said that 'women had to be made over by man so that she might become more acceptable to him.' And he also admitted that—wait a minute, I have the exact quote here—he said that 'since modern psychology is not masculine but derived from our neurotic type of man, a great deal of its terminology originated from misinterpretation of women in term's of man's sexual ideology.' Which simply means that a woman who goes to a male therapist—no matter how sympathetic or well meaning he is—has to consider where he's coming from. What's his professional training? What's his personal background and acculturation? And even beyond that—what's buried in his unconscious?"

"Then her only hope is a female therapist?"

"Not necessarily, Isabel. I mean not *all* female therapists will fill the bill. Because, as Broverman indicates, most female clinicians accept the same old orthodox Freudian and neo-Freudian notions about women. So right now I'd have to say that only a liberated female therapist can adequately treat another female."

"That means you," said Rachel. "You're the kind of clinician that's needed."

242

"I'm not so sure, Rachel. I've been out of the field for years, and all kinds of changes have taken place."

"Take a few refresher courses."

"I guess I could. But that's not my principal concern. I'm mostly bothered about my own capabilities. I might not be able to handle a therapeutic relationship anymore. I'm liable to freeze in the middle of a session. Or even come apart. As a matter of fact, I've been having this strange dream lately—more of a nightmare really— in which I'm conducting a Rorschach test for a female patient. Everything goes well until I hand her the sixth card and ask her what she sees in the inkblot. Hesitating a few moments, she finally tells me it's a dead cat, and I suddenly get terribly angry with her. *'It's not dead!'* I shout at her. *'How can you say that? It's not dead at all!'* Then, still mouthing those words, I wake up gasping for air—but luckily not agitated enough to disturb my husband."

"Have you told him about the dream?"

"Not yet I haven't. And maybe I won't ever tell him. I'm afraid he'd discourage me from returning to work. He might think I've lost all my objectivity—that I've become too subjective. Female clinicians are frequently accused of that."

"But, Selma, just a few weeks ago you yourself told us that most psychiatrists and analysts are pretty neurotic, that their own emotional hangups make them more sensitive to other people's neuroses."

"That's true, Isabel. But they're somehow able to sublimate them and to achieve some measure of objectivity."

"You mean that sphinx look," said Rachel. "That cross between boredom and indifference—or just high-priced daydreaming."

"Probably all three," agreed Selma. "But there's got to be some degree of self-control to fake that blank

243

expression, and I'm not sure I have that kind of self-control anymore."

"Of course you do," said Ruth. "You're just out of practice. It'll all come back to you. Just wait and see. All you need is a little practice, Selma."

"Well—now that you've mentioned it—I might as well confess that I *have* been practicing these past few months. But in a very indirect way. Mostly an observational thing."

"That's wonderful, Selma. But where do you meet your patients?"

"Right here. But they're not exactly patients. In fact, they're not patients at all."

"Then what do you call them?"

"I don't call them anything. They're just friends. And their names are Rachel, Trudy, Ruth, Graciela, Jan, and Isabel . . ."

"You mean *us?* You've been analyzing *us?*"

"But how can you? You haven't given us any tests or asked any questions."

"Well, it hasn't been that kind of psychological analysis. Just casual observation. I hadn't intended to get into this thing, but I got sort of compulsive. So after every meeting I've dictated a few observations on each one of you, basing my tentative conclusion—well, not really conclusions, more like hunches—based on my previous experience and training. I wasn't going to mention it, but I've been feeling kind of guilty about it; that's why I'm telling you now. With deep apologies, of course. It wasn't very kosher."

"No need for apologies," said Isabel. "No one's been harmed."

Several voices expressed agreement with her during the ensuing babble, and finally Rachel asked the inevitable question: "And what were your final conclusions about us?"

"No conclusions really—just a few tentative hunches, most of which I kept changing from one meeting to another. And that's what bothers me: I mean my inability to judge people more accurately. Now I don't mean *judge* in the conventional sense—not at all. That would be awfully presumptuous. *Appraise* is what I meant. But whatever you call it, I've been terribly erratic in my hunches."

"Maybe it's us," said Trudy. "Perhaps we've been changing so rapidly that you couldn't possibly reach any firm conclusions—or hunches, if that's what you want to call them."

"That's possible, I guess. But I'm afraid it was mostly a matter of faulty judgment on my part. Perhaps I've been too damned subjective."

"Now you're really piquing my curiosity, sweetie," said Rachel with a half chuckle. "What were some of those hunches?"

"I'd rather not say," Selma demurred. "Most of them were silly or presumptuous. And certainly premature, Rachel."

"Silly or not, I'd like to hear them."

"So would I!" chorused several others.

"But they were so erroneous—so totally off base in retrospect."

"I'd still like to hear them."

"Okay. If that's what you want. But I'll give you only a few examples. Now let's start with you, Rachel. . . ."

"I'm listening."

"Well, let's go back to our first meeting: When you jokingly referred to yourself as a 'black *shiksa*' and later told us about your son's problems as a black teen-ager in a white school, I quickly assumed that your being black was the primary force in your emotional makeup. Then a couple of meetings later I thought it might be your

245

part-time lesbianism. Yet most of the time—I mean in all our other discussions—I got very few indications that either of those factors was the dominant influence. It was your status as a woman that seemed to shape most of your emotional and intellectual life. But now I'm beginning to feel that my appraisals were too damned subjective, that I've been pushing my own psyche into yours, that my own feminist bias will inevitably—"

"But why must you find a primary force?" asked Rachel. "Perhaps all of those factors are primary from time to time. At least that's the way I see them. And feel them. So maybe your hunches have been right all along. Your real difficulty was in trying to fix priorities where there aren't any."

"Because I'm looking for an easy analysis," said Selma. "Which could be laziness. Or, more probably, I'm subconsciously afraid to tackle a really complex problem, where there are too many variables spinning around. Lack of confidence perhaps. . . . Yet I'm dead sure of one thing. Which applies to all of us."

"What's that?"

"That economic insecurity is one of the root causes of our dilemma. That we've got to start earning some of our own money. And that's why I'm so happy that most of us are going back to work or back to college to prepare for work. Because, no matter what gains we make on such matters as abortion on demand, political equality, educational parity, or anything else, we're still going to be oppressed until we finally achieve dollar parity. Without money of our own, we can't be liberated."

"Which is true of all oppressed groups," added Rachel. "Including most blacks."

"We're getting off the track again," said Graciela. "Selma had started telling us about her tentative hunches, and I'd like to hear more."

"Okay—just a couple more, 'cause it's getting pretty

246

late. Now let's take my hundred-percent-wrong hunch about Ruth. From our first meeting, I had the impression that she was the most timid and conservative member of our group, the one least likely to change from the status quo. But she was the very first one to make a radical move when she filed suit for a divorce. So you see, Ruth, I've been completely mistaken in my appraisal of you."

"So have I, Selma. Six months ago I wouldn't have dreamed of divorcing Walter, no matter how unhappy I was. And if I hadn't joined this group, I might have stayed with him. You've given me lots of moral support, and that's why I hate to see us drifting apart."

"Drifting apart?"

"That's the way it looks, Selma. Two weeks ago Jan dropped out. And tonight we've been told that Trudy, Graciela, and Isabel are dropping out. Which leaves only three of the original seven."

"But my absence will be only temporary—I hope," said Trudy.

"Same here," said Graciela.

"So will mine," added Isabel. "I'll be coming back in a couple of months."

"That being the case," said Selma, "I'd suggest that we suspend our meetings for two or three months. Then take it from there. But I hope we'll be seeing each other for lunch or dinner occasionally."

"Or maybe a drink," said Ruth. "I hate to drink alone."

XIII

Reckonings

ON the following Sunday morning, as he carefully braised some mushrooms for a special brunch, John suddenly asked his wife why she had been so moody during the past few days.

"Something's been bothering you," he said. "You've been sort of mopey."

"I guess so," she conceded, pursing her lips and frowning as she poured herself a second cup of coffee and leaned back on the window seat of the breakfast nook. "We've come to a turning point in our rap sessions, and I'm not sure what turn we'll take. Into a dead end maybe."

"How so?"

"We seem to be breaking up," she said. "One of our members dropped out for good about two weeks ago when her husband gave her a *macho* ultimatum. And last Thursday night three others announced they'd have to quit coming. They all said it would be temporary, but I've got a feeling it'll be permanent."

"That's too bad. It really is. You seemed to be getting a good deal out of your sessions. But what did you mean by *macho ultimatum?*"

"That was Jan's husband. He put it very bluntly to her: quit us or quit him."

"But why?"

"Because he felt threatened by her sudden inde-

248

pendence. She'd like to leave him, but there're certain complications that—well, I really shouldn't talk about it."

"Okay, I understand. I didn't mean to pry or anything like that . . . more cream?"

There was a long silence again, his wife vacantly staring out the window with her cup resting on the sill while John busied himself with the sizzling buttered mushrooms, now and then pausing to glance her way. He had usually respected her silences. Or perhaps feared them. They so often seemed like huge chasms that could never be bridged or closed again, measureless gaps of psychic isolation that disturbed him far more than even their most brutal confrontations. "When you argue or fight," he subsequently told me, "there's at least some involvement on your part, but you can never tell when she goes silent on you; that could mean anything." Consequently, he had generally forced himself to "quietly ride the tide" when she got that way. But on this particular morning, perhaps prompted by the reference to Jan wanting to leave her husband, John was finally impelled to ask the inevitable question.

"How about you?"

She turned from the window with a puzzled look in her eyes. "Pardon?"

"Have you ever wanted to leave me?"

"Occasionally, John. But not lately. I guess most women, even those who are presumably happy, think about divorce now and then. We've certainly talked about it in our group—at almost every session. Not necessarily bitching about our husbands, mind you, but just wondering if marriage is a viable institution. I mean the way it's presently set up. I'm sure a lot of men ask the very same question."

"They do, all right. Though probably not as often as women do."

249

"That's because marriage is different for men. It's not quite as confining . . . or oppressive."

"Probably not," he said. "But what other arrangement can you make? Especially with kids. And even without children, I wouldn't care to live alone."

"Neither would I," she admitted. "Though I guess just living with someone—I mean without the legal bit—can eventually develop into something just as oppressive as marriage. But beyond that, you've got the problem of being a mother. Which might conceivably be the worst difficulty in any marriage. Yet how can any of us—once we've been exposed to that old motherhood myth—how can we ever escape that damned compulsion or desire or phobia or whatever it is? That's where I'm really hooked, John."

"Hooked?"

"Well, maybe *hooked* is not the word I'm looking for. What I'm trying to say is that I might someday leave this house. Leave both you and the kids. Not because I don't love you or don't love them. Because I really do—at least most or maybe only half the time. Yet I may need to find out if there's some other way for me to feel like a whole person."

"But you are. You're as complete a person as anyone I know, Poochie. Certainly more complete than I am. Or will ever be."

"Now you're trying to con me. But before you go any further, John, you'd better watch those mushrooms —they're liable to burn."

As so frequently happens, in their immediate preoccupation with the stuffing and baking of six fist-sized mushrooms, they were soon diverted to more casual topics of conversation, eventually focusing on her nephew's dropping out of Yale at the very beginning of his freshman year.

"It seems so sad and wasteful," she said.

"And a little frightening," he added. "There's a basic failure somewhere. Either in the kids or the colleges. Or maybe both."

"It's more likely our educational systems, John. They're not keeping up. Everything's changing, and they're staying put, most of them. That's what makes me a little dubious about going back."

"Going back?"

"To college, I mean. I've been thinking of going back to the university for my degree and then going on for a master's in speech therapy. Back to where I was headed before I met you."

"Sounds like a great idea. You ought to start right away. There's still time to register for the fall term."

"Yes, I know. But I'm a little scared."

"Scared of what?"

"Of everything. Myself mostly. It's been a long time since I cracked a book."

"Nonsense. That's sheer nonsense. You read as much as anyone I know. You'd be far ahead of most of those kids."

"That's a different kind of reading from school reading. You don't have to take notes. Or tests. That's where I'm liable to freeze, John. Taking tests or answering questions in class."

"You can do it, Poochie. I know you can. You've always been a good student. So quit downgrading yourself. Women are always doing that. And please forgive me if that sounds sexist to you, but I think it's true. My mother and sister were always doing that, and pretty soon they quit trying. In fact, they never started."

"I know that, John. That's one of our biggest problems as females. We've been psyched into thinking we're inferior to men, and that's. . . ."

"But you're not, damn it! You've been sold a crock of shit. At inflated prices. And I'm awfully sorry about all

251

that. I guess we're all to blame, but somewhere, somehow we've got to stop this nonsense. So you've got to go back to college, and you've got to stop downgrading yourself. You're an intelligent human being, for God's sake!"

"That's nice of you, John. That's really beautiful. And I know you mean it. But I'm still scared, and I'm going to need all the encouragement I can get. That's why I've been so moody since our meeting last Thursday night. I don't want our group to break up so soon. We've been so good for each other, so quick to support each other. All of us. You can't imagine what it means to have that kind of support, that kind of *esprit de corps*. I guess that's why so many people secretly envy the special closeness between black people."

"I've sort of sensed that thing between women," he said. "You get a hint of it in *Ms*, which, incidentally, is a damned good magazine. I just got a subscription for my sister."

"You did?"

"That's right. She'll get the very next issue in her mailbox."

"What will her husband say about that?"

"He'll probably blow his stack. But I don't give a damn what that bastard says. Now, if you think I'm a male chauvinist pig, you should see Roger in action."

"But I've never said you were a pig, John. Male chauvinist perhaps—but seldom a pig. As a matter of fact, I think you've come a long way these past few months. So have I. At least I hope so. I had gotten so tired of hating."

"Hating?"

"That's right, John—hating. I hated you, I hated the kids, and (mostly) I hated myself. And it was so damned exhausting, because I'd been trying to hide that hatred all these years and feeling guilty because of it. But it was getting so explosive, so frightening. Then suddenly,

252

during the first few meetings of our consciousness-raising group, I let it go—like a boiler blasting steam. We all did. And it was really scary. All that hatred and frustration pouring out! But after a while we started to simmer down; we got more perspective, more insight. That's when I realized that my hatred of you—that god-awful continuous resentment—was less personal than I had originally thought. It wasn't you as *you* that I resented; it was you as husband, as the domineering symbol of marriage. And of course I had also been hating myself for submitting to a lot of crap that I couldn't possibly accept in the long run. But over and above all that—if any of this makes sense to you—where the pressures of motherhood and wifehood and the unbearable need to love and to be loved by you and the kids. All that longing to be part of a unit, part of an idealized family, mixed with a desperate need to escape from that ·very same unit—to assert myself as a separate independent being."

"That's a pretty tough dilemma," said John, feeling ineffably sad and helpless.

"I know it is. But I'm determined to find some kind of balance between those needs. There has to be some way . . . and I want you to help me find it."

"I'll try. But you'll have to help me to understand how I can help you—how I can help myself as well. Sometimes you get into areas (emotional and psychological) that I've never traveled before. Out of fear or ignorance—who knows? I guess they're areas quite familiar to women, yet totally alien to men."

"Could be," she said. "Especially when women really get down to the nitty-gritty, the way we have in our rap sessions. You should have heard some of the things that were said, John. Absolutely amazing. Sometimes I wished that I had bugged myself with one of those hidden recording devices that are used by informers for the FBI, those little electronic microphones that you can carry in a purse or attach to your brassiere. I could have kept a permanent record of what we said. It seems like such a waste to lose all those valuable ideas and expressions of real emotion. Such a loss."

"It certainly is," said John, offering her the last mushroom in the platter.